Play
the Game

Making the Most of Your
One Wild and Precious Life

First published by O Books, 2009

O Books is an imprint of John Hunt Publishing Ltd., The Bothy, Deershot Lodge, Park Lane, Ropley,
Hants, SO24 0BE, UK
office1@o-books.net
www.o-books.net

Distribution in:

UK and Europe
Orca Book Services
orders@orcabookservices.co.uk
Tel: 01202 665432 Fax: 01202 666219
Int. code (44)

USA and Canada
NBN
custserv@nbnbooks.com
Tel: 1 800 462 6420 Fax: 1 800 338 4550

Australia and New Zealand
Brumby Books
sales@brumbybooks.com.au
Tel: 61 3 9761 5535 Fax: 61 3 9761 7095

Far East (offices in Singapore, Thailand,
Hong Kong, Taiwan)
Pansing Distribution Pte Ltd
kemal@pansing.com
Tel: 65 6319 9939 Fax: 65 6462 5761

South Africa
Alternative Books
altbook@peterhyde.co.za
Tel: 021 555 4027 Fax: 021 447 1430

Text copyright Corinne Williams 2008

Design: Stuart Davies

ISBN: 978 1 84694 213 6

A CIP catalogue record for this book is available
from the British Library.

Printed by Digital Book Print

O Books operates a distinctive and ethical publishing philosophy in
all areas of its business, from its global network of authors to
production and worldwide distribution.
This book is produced on FSC certified stock, within ISO14001
standards. The printer plants sufficient trees each year through
the Woodland Trust to absorb the level of emitted carbon in
its production.

Play
the Game

Making the Most of Your
One Wild and Precious Life

Corinne Williams

BOOKS

Winchester, UK
Washington, USA

Mary Oliver is an American poet who explores her place in the world and celebrates the beauty of Nature in her poetry. Read some if you get the chance! The subtitle for this book was inspired by her poem The Summer Day that she ends by asking,

'Tell me, what is it you plan to do with your one wild and precious life?'

CONTENTS

Preface

When I was five, my favourite place was my den in amongst the tall dark trees at the bottom of the garden. This was my own world where all was safe and well. Outside however, the bigger, wider world was a strange planet to me. I was always peering out from behind my wonky fringe searching for something I might recognise, trying to work out what made people tick and just what this Life thing was all about.

I kind of had an inkling that what was on the surface of things was only hiding worlds of interesting stuff beneath, and so began my exploration of what Being Alive on this Earth might mean for me. It took me a while, but I discovered that I had choices, that I could choose how to feel and how my Life could be. I really wanted a Life that was fun, creative and magical, and it now is!

The ideas and tools and tips I offer to you here were once passed on to me, perhaps by a friend or a teacher, or in a book I found useful or in a dream that woke me up and made me fall out of bed as I scrambled for my pen to write it down. They are here because they are simple and they really do help to make playing this game we call Life a lot more fun.

Within each chapter are exercises to play around with. You might want to read through the book first and come back to them, or experiment as you go along. Make this book your own – scribble ideas in the margins, doodle in the spaces if you want to. Dip into it as and when you feel drawn to it.

What I hope is that you find something in here that reminds you that you are here, living this Life, for a really good reason. That who you are is just who you were always meant to be, and that you have a place and a purpose on this Earth that is uniquely yours.

Enjoy!

Corinne

Chapter 1

Advance to Go

'It's just a ride, and we can change it any time we want.'
Bill Hicks

Happy birthday!

You're dead excited. It's as if you've been waiting for a lifetime and here it is, in your hands. It's brand new, this game, and you can hardly wait to play it. You don't stop to read the instructions, they're lost in the frenzy to get into the game, but you just dive straight into it, and it's incredible! There's so much to take in, so much to experience that your senses are thrilled and amazed and confused all at once. It's like riding on the biggest rollercoaster you've ever seen – the colours streaming past you, the blur of sounds, everything seems so real. It's so much fun, you never want to get off.

And then, well, then you do. The game is cool, but you want to know how to get onto the next level, want to do something a bit different, try out some other skills, but you can't seem to find the instructions and can't remember where you put them. Everyone's giving you all this advice, and some of it helps, it really does, but some of it is worse than useless and it's all getting a bit frustrating and difficult and suddenly you're tired and fed up and don't really fancy playing any more thanks, but someone says you have to carry on, they say you have to keep on going right till The Very End.

But that's just Life, isn't it?

Your Life, that is.

What?

Well, let's assume that you've been building up to this thing we call Life for ages, just like the game you really wanted to play. You've been planning and choosing the Life that best fits your every need and desire. The design is superb, the layout just what you'd hoped for.

Now, a bit further on down the line, there you are, floating around in your own little warm and cosy world, feeling pretty pleased with yourself (you've just perfected this fantastic roly poly baby-in-space move) when suddenly you're being squeezed and Eek! I mean really squeeeeeeeeeeeezed and you're getting all tired and it's not very nice actually and it's all dark when suddenly it's not because it's LIGHT LIGHT LIGHT and who turned up the volume? It's all LOUD and Look! Look at this! And that! And what's this? Who's that?

Good Grief.

Welcome to the World.

Busy, isn't it?

So you've been born, and remember that Life is a game that you really, really wanted to play, so it's a bit of a shock when you emerge unable to communicate your excitement except in these weird squawking sounds and worse still, instead of handing you a fresh and easy-to-follow copy of The Rules that might tell you what On Earth is going on and what to do next, some woman in a white coat wraps you in a scratchy towel and whisks you off to be weighed. This was not quite what you had in mind.

You're probably feeling a mixture of excitementfearwonder-coldapprehension which is rather a strange sensation, because let's not forget that till quite recently you were an altogether more relaxed little dude, chilling out in your own little pad, floating about and well, yeah, baby! just being...

And in all the rush and noise and things everywhere to look at and touch and smell and taste, it's no real surprise that that you kind of forget that you came here to play the Game of Life that you'd spent so long choosing, that you really made the choice to come here, that you have all the bits you need to do all the things you wanted to do.

Unsurprising that there are millions of these Games of Life lying all over the place, unopened, unused, and growing dusty. Maybe you've just forgotten, what with all the rush and mayhem, that in order to play properly and effortlessly and with all the fun you knew was possible, you had to learn a few things first, remember some important information, and this Being Born thing, and the Growing Up business that followed were all part of that.

Hum. Maybe.

But hey! It's enough for now just taking it all in and learning all the stuff that's important like who's who for a start, and what happens when you poke the cat in the eye and the fact that you absolutely hate yogurt and even at this early stage in your career as an experimental artist with an aversion to dairy foods you can let everyone know by flinging a bowl full of it onto the floor which creates a fantastic pattern and makes your dad sigh and your older sister laugh. Oh yes.

There's loads of stuff to learn and lots of it is really good fun, which is cool. And some things you learn on your own (see above) and other things people tell you. It's really useful to have these guys around because they can tell you it's dangerous to practise your roly-poly move *(Wow! Where did you learn that??)* at the top of the stairs, and even though it looks ridiculous, a banana *is* a real food and actually quite delicious, and so on and so far, so good.

It seems to you that these people around you are the cleverest, wisest, most powerfullest folks in the Universe. And if you're lucky, they're kind and funny and teach you the best things they know.

Surely they know every rule in the book?

Tying up your shoes might seem easy now, but cast your mind back a few years to when just getting hold of a glow-in-the-dark jumbo lace required a dexterity you supposed forever out of reach until someone sat you down and spent a happyfrustratinginfuriatingwonderfulsuccessful EUREKA!!! moment revealing to you the magic that your very own fingers might weave around your teeny size twelves.

Make a list of the biggest Eureka! moments in your Life so far.

Who taught you to ride your bike/eat spaghetti/say hello in Norwegian?
Remember who was there with you to apply plasters/wipe up sauce/snigger because you'd just announced, and with a perfect Norwegian accent, that your dog Rufus enjoys scuba diving in his spare time...

Well done to you, and big thanks to them.

Chapter 2

Learning the Rules

'Learning is finding out what you already know.'
Richard Bach

So we learn by experimenting (the orange juice on your cornflakes idea? How come that never caught on, I wonder...?) and by being shown.

We're like little radars too, picking up signals about what is 'good' for us to do, and what is 'bad', usually by observing the looks on people's faces and their reactions to the things we do. Let's face it, we've only just got here so it's only natural that we want to make friends and fit in. We want to be 'good'. We don't want to be getting on everyone's nerves and be asked to leave early now, do we?

So watching and listening are useful and all this is great if you're watching good stuff, positive stuff, because when we're young and our eyes are wide they eat everything up without knowing what's yummy and what might make us feel yuck (it was the cornflake and juice bit that led me here...) and if we watch something happening often enough we tend to think, 'Ah! So that's how it's done.' And do the same.

So let's imagine then that, as well as all the good stuff, you learn, for example, that spiders are the most dangerous form of life on the planet. And that if you ever see one, it's a Rule to scream, feel very afraid and wave your arms in the air.

You also learn that mushrooms are disgusting. You've never actually tasted one, but no one likes them, do they? Yuk.

And did you know that the two kids who live down the road who always look really scruffy aren't very nice and if they ever walk past you and say 'All right?' you have to ignore them?

Oh, and it's not good to show off and show people the pictures you've drawn as if they're something special because you just look big-headed and let's face it, they're not really that good anyway. Who do you think you are, some kind of artist? Guffaw!

Ooer. Some of the things you're learning don't feel quite right, and just for fun, let's see how things would turn out if you followed just those four Rules...

For starters, you'd be really hungry that night when you and your mates go camping and the only thing on the menu is the cold mushroom lasagne that your best friend's Auntie Doreen popped into their rucksack just in case the gas ran out or something. Which it did.

You can't really enjoy the night-time frolics round the campfire on the same trip because someone suggests Pictionary by torchlight and you freeze afraid inside and well, no, you don't really want to play because well, you can't draw. You don't know why, you just can't.

You don't get a wink of sleep later, not only because your stomach is growling like a huge and hungry bear, but because you're terrified that the spiders and other creepy crawly things you've been warned about will all crawl creepily into your sleeping bag in the night and probably kill you.

And when the car breaks down in the rain and you're walking

back to the garage someone thought they saw in the last village, you get soaked by the tidal wave created by the red Mini that races past you.

So what have those Rules done for you then?
Not only do you end up The Last Person Anyone Would Want To Go Camping With - Ever - you've had a really rubbish time and arrive home feeling cold and hungry and embarrassed and angry, and looking mournfully out of the window you catch sight of a red Mini that reminds you of it all over again. Sigh.

(The fact that it *is* the same red Mini and belongs to one of the two brothers down the road who was up in the hills this same weekend visiting his sick granny, and if you'd made friends with him years ago he would have given you and your mates a lift, no problem, cos he's like that, is something I won't mention because, well, I don't want to rub it in and frankly, I think you've suffered enough. But do you get the point?)

It all might have been *sooooooo* different...

Dear Mum,
Found this really unusual species of tree spider yesterday. (See sketch.)
The car broke down but we got a lift from some mates - lucky, eh? They took us to this great spot they knew and we found loads of edible mushrooms.
I'll bring some home.
See you!
Love,
A. Camper xxx

Ho hum. So, all those crazy habits, the negative beliefs about yourself and other people. You certainly didn't start out with them, but you've picked them up from somewhere along the way.

Who taught you that it's pathetic to cry?

Who once told you that people who live on the street are lazy, it's their own fault?

And this isn't about blaming anyone else for how you feel/act/dress right now.

In fact, they might have taught you some useful lessons along the way by making you wonder and think hard about certain things.

It doesn't even matter if you can't remember how you learned these things, or who taught you to behave like you sometimes do, without even thinking about it. It's enough to realise that most of what we believe about ourselves, and a lot of the stuff that we say and do is thanks to all we've watched and listened to and absorbed like the little spongy creatures that we are. Parents, carers, friends, TV sets, teachers, brothers, bus drivers...We're surrounded by them and so it's not surprising that we end up taking in a lot of what they say and do.

Take teachers, for example. (An odd example perhaps, but then they're an oddly interesting breed.) Teachers all over the world really do gasp in horror as the phrase 'Simmer down, Year 9...' passes their lips for the first time. Nobody really knows what makes them say it, but would you choose consciously to ask someone to 'simmer down'?

Simmer down?! What does it all mean, apart from them having to wait, understandably, for their class to stop sniggering... Perhaps their teachers had once said it to them; perhaps they felt it was expected of them in their teacherish role; perhaps their Year 9 class really did resemble a bubbling bean and vegetable stew coming to the boil (although unless they had consumed something stronger than the usual cheese sarnie at lunch, this one is unlikely...).

And actually, underneath the strange and bewildering exterior, your teacher still possesses the same mischievous streak she did when she was fourteen years old, and it's that part of her that silently shrieks, "You what?!" when some odd phrase flies out of her mouth...

Ever opened your mouth and had words that really belong to your mum/some soap character/your Peruvian pen friend fly out? It's happened to us all.

Maybe it was the way you dressed or acted that really belonged to someone else?

Remember that experience here. How did it feel then, and how does it feel now to look at it?

Maybe you learned something, if only that lunchtimes might have been more fun that year if you'd had something other than raspberry yogurt, chips and beans - 'But, urghhh, not the green ones, thanks!' - just because your friend Vicky did. Every single day.

Or it might have been something bigger and more important. It'll come to you.

'All the world's a stage, and all the men and women, merely players...'*

What roles do you play in your life? Think about the different costumes you put on in different situations, the different words you use in different places and with different characters you share a scene or two with. You might be one sort of person with close friends and play a very different role when you go to your granny's for tea.

Wonder at how versatile and talented you are, adapting to all the different situations you face over the course of just one day. Are there any roles that you feel you've played for long enough? Any roles you'd like to drop now? Maybe you'd like to try out for a new part?

Spend a moment thinking about how it feels to take off the masks at the end of the day, when the curtain has swished its way across the stage and you can relax, alone.

Who is it that looks back at you in the bathroom mirror? Who is it that lies in bed just before you fall asleep?

How does it feel to be You, without the expectation of others who see you as the paper girl/ quiet boy in class/ mummy's baby/ troublemaker on the bus?

Sometimes we play so many roles that it can be difficult to switch off at the end of the day, and sometimes, without other people to reflect back an image of ourselves to us, it's hard to know what it means to be truly ourselves.

What does it mean to be truly, authentically, absolutely You?

---

* William Shakespeare, someone who knew a thing or two about Life, left us this to think on.

And if you find this a difficult question to answer, you're not alone. Zillions of people have been asking themselves that same simple question since time began, and much beetling of brows and fizzing of brains is the start of the long journey to find out. It might be a long one, but it's worth making, and the intention to discover who You really are is absolutely necessary to living your very own Real Life.

Real Life, anyone? Then step this way...

(Amazing that so few people actually take up this invitation, even though everyone gets one. Least that means there's no queue, unlike the crush for the Sleep Your Way Through Life party – it's totally packed, but *what* a nightmare...)

Chapter 3

You Little Diamond

'Magic is believing in yourself. If you can do that, you can make anything happen.'
Goethe

Henry David Thoreau, a person noted for his appreciation of the natural beauty of the world, suggested we 'Simplify!' and who are we to argue with such sound advice?

Clearing away some of the heavy, negative images we have of ourselves really is possible and is vital if we are to live a lighter, more positive life, and we'll be exploring ways to do that, ways that really work and which people have been using for thousands of years but most of us seem to have forgotten along the way.

To start with, it's time to clear some of that clutter. Yep, the old comics in the back of the wardrobe, the Spiderman underpants that you wore when you were seven, the bottle of green eerie liquid that could be anything, lurking under the bed. It all has to go.

By throwing away the stuff that is no longer useful to you – and this applies just as much to negative thoughts as to the Spiderman undies – you create a space for some new, good stuff to make its way into your life. Recycle as much as you can, maybe sending off your unwanted things to a charity shop that might then raise some cash for a good cause. Doing something useful doesn't only benefit you but in some way always benefits others too.

You could get together with some friends and have a sale to raise money and do something really fun with the proceeds. Be creative. It's much more fun than being stuck in your room unable to move because everywhere you look is mess and dust and scary things growing in old coffee mugs. In that situation our focus is pulled away from anything useful by a million little distractions and this can make our heads really confused and tire us out even before we get out of bed in the morning. You might have created this mess, but you have everything you need (and one of those groovy feather dusters, if you're lucky) to create the more positive and healthy environment you want to live in now.

Get busy with the Hoover, dust down a few surfaces that do actually exist under all that clutter and see how it feels for yourself.

Afterwards, you might want to make it special and mark the moment by having a shower to wash away any dust and grime that's jumped off the window sill and all over you, and come back into your room, seeing it with new eyes. This is your place to start afresh in, a place where your dreams will have room to grow in.

Now, just as an experiment, choose your favourite pen, one that makes your writing as purple/turquoise/shiny as it can be, and write down as many positive things about yourself as you can.

Be specific.
I helped my mum set up the web site for her new business/I enjoy listening to the younger kids read/I make a mean cheese and gherkin sarnie/I love to paint in oils...

List all the things you do well, the skills you have, the qualities you feel are positive.

Keep going for 5 minutes. Time yourself, and....Go!

Cool!

You are a pretty amazing human being! Not everyone can gargle a selection of Tom Jones' Greatest Hits whilst balancing on one leg, you know, and the person who can grow potatoes that resemble members of their family and, what's more, serve them perfectly cooked in a lemon butter dressing (the potatoes, that is), is a rare find.

Feel good about these things. Put this list in a safe place and refer to it often, especially in those times when you feel a bit low, just to remind yourself that it is possible to see things in a positive light and when you need to remember how gorgeous/creative/important you are to this world!

Now, smiley people, on a separate page, please make a list of all the things about your life that you believe aren't quite so good, the bits you don't feel so positive about.

You've got 5 minutes...and, heavens, you've started already...

...three, two, one, Stop! STOP!! STOP!!!!

Phew.

Bet I know which is the longer list. And bet I know which was the easiest to write, because for some spooky reason, most of us, when first trying out this little experiment, do tend to have a longer not-so-positive list. Yep.

And if yours is a l-o-n-g list, (and they can run and run, believe me), then that's a lot of not-so-positive stuff to be carrying around every day. It wears you out, makes you tired.

Okay then, now you're feeling all grouchy and annoyed and asking, 'Just what am I doing focusing on all the rubbishy bits about me anyway?'
'Just what is the point of all this?'

Excellent questions, and would you believe me if I told you that the rubbishy bits aren't actually *you* at all? And I admit, it sounds weird, but stay with me here…

Let's imagine a strong slab of metal, a magnet as sleek as a seal. It's untarnished and wonderful. Then, as magnets do, it attracts some stuff. First it's some shiny little silvery bits and pieces but that's okay, you can still see it's a magnet and it looks sort of interesting like that anyway. However, before long, it's covered in rusty tin cans and all sorts of rubbish until one day, all you can see is this heavy mass of junky stuff.

Someone who knew could get rid of all that, pull off the layers bit by bit until its beauty was restored.
You can see that, can't you?

Then there's the diamond ring that fell into a honey pot that got thrown in the bin bag that ended up in a landfill and got covered in mud and was eventually buried until years and years later, when the site had been bought by some mindful person and transformed into a garden, it was dug up and…wow! They found a diamond!!

And remember the little blanket with the yellow ducks on that you took with you everywhere, and I mean *every*where, that started off pure and white and ended up unrecognisable and in the dog's basket? Remember the day it got thrown in the wash by accident and although your mum went mad because it turned the white socks grey, it came out restored by some miracle and you found it and felt so happy, so secure, it was like meeting up with an old friend?

Well, you started off as pure and sweet as that. As rare and beautiful as that diamond and as strong and powerful as the biggest magnet in the world. Only, along the way, we all pick up stuff that means that somehow, some of that beauty and power and sweetness and intelligence and creativity and confidence and the very very essence of Us is obscured. We can't make it out as well any more.

'Oh. Great. That's just great,' I hear several hundred of you sigh. Heavily.

'What am I supposed to do with that fantastic piece of knowledge?'

Well, if you're aware of something, then it's a lot easier to do something about it.

If you're aware that quite a lot of the beliefs you have about yourself and others are simply holding you back and are not so much more than a load of heavy baggage, you can decide to put that baggage down. Open it up if you want to, rifle through the murkier bits if you must, but then you might decide that you really don't need that stuff any more. And continue, feeling strangely, but Hey! wonderfully lighter and more positive.

By zooming in on all the bits you've acquired over the however many years you've been doing your thing on this rather fantastic Earthy planet we call home, and identifying them, you can sort out where they came from and decide which bits need shining up and which bits you can safely let go of.

Basically, we just choose to let go of all the rubbish.

(Well, why didn't you say...?)

So. Here goes. A first step...

Tear out the separate rubbishy-bits page. Do this bravely, with a flourish. If you could arrange it, a fanfare of trumpets would be good.
Rip into as many pieces as possible. (Perhaps a drum roll...? Fireworks..?)
Say goodbye. And really mean this.
Goodbye to believing that people like you are rubbish at maths/shouldn't make a fuss/will never be what in your heart of hearts you really want to be.
Goodbye forever.

Dispose of safely.*

(And this isn't about getting unrealistic – sometimes it's useful to focus briefly on something we find difficult to do because that's just the area we need to spend a bit of time developing, and some people are always going to be better at some things than others, which is perfectly okay. It's when we start limiting ourselves by trying to force ourselves into a shape that doesn't really fit us just so that we might fit in with the crowd, or by believing that our own strengths and aptitudes, the things we are naturally good at, are worthless, that the problems start.)

By saying goodbye to those negative beliefs you've written down, the ones that make you feel heavy and tired and small just

---

* Top Tip: Paper will eventually make great compost – recycle your rubbish and grow flowers (or root vegetables in the shape of minor celebrities – *see above*) instead.

thinking about them, you're taking the first exhilarating step as the real YOU!

So, go on, look around you. Listen. Are the colours brighter, the birds singing, people dancing in the summer sun and running up to shake your hand? No?! They're not?

Well, I did say this was the *first* step, but it really is the most important.
This is your own decision, your choice, your right to make a difference to how you feel, and to the Life you are living right now, as you scratch your nose/take a sip of water/read this.

Hello you!

Chapter 4

Mind Games

'I shut my eyes in order to see.'
Paul Gauguin

Our minds are pretty amazing things. Born to think, they do what they do incredibly well, almost *too* well at times. Maybe there should be a little sticker with the words 'Too much thinking can be bad for you' in sparkly letters/bold type/fluorescent ink on the inside where we can see it with our eyes closed to remind us to stop, just every now and again.

Try it now. Not the writing on the inside of your eyelids thing. Too messy. Just stop thinking.

'....................stop thinking, thinking stop bee doo bee doo red amber green little creatures stuck forever in amber, dinosaurs and all that, millions of species lost forever, like my English book, I really have no idea where that went and I just get blamed for everything - it's just not fair! It must be somewhere, it exists somewhere and I don't know where...it can't just dematerialise, can it? Can it? What does that mean anyway? Wish I could just disappear sometimes...disappear where to? Atoms flung to the farthest reaches of the universe ha ha! so not entirely actually gone completely then, cos if there's still an atom, a teeny bit of me left does that mean that I still am, somewhere? Ooch. My brain hurts...I can hear an aeroplane wheeeeeee... stop thinking......stop thinking.........easy peasy, yep, think I did pretty well there......'

Ahem.

Difficult, isn't it?

Our minds are meant to think, and thoughts are what they do best, so you're not going to be able to switch them off, just like that. But there are little tricks you can play with your mind to get it to take a break, and our minds love any sort of game, so they can get pretty good at them.

First, a pair of white gloves is essential, as they can make shuffling the pack of cards a little easier. The rabbit in the hat needs careful coaxing to appear at the right moment, but it's amazing what you can achieve with a carrot stick and years of determination...

Oh dear. A little focus is what's needed here, methinks.

Focus.

Drawing your mind's eye back to one thing, reining it in a bit, and reminding it just who is in control here, because, yes, hard to believe I know, but you are actually capable of being in control of the wild horses that seem to gallop freely and at random across the vast and dusty outback that is your mind. (And don't worry. It's not just *your* mind, they're all at it...)

Try this.
Breathe in, breathe out. Breathe in, breathe out. Breathe in, breathe out.

Yep, it's that easy.

Breathing, as most of us know, is pretty essential if we want to get on in life. What most of us don't know is how to do it really well.

Be aware of how you are breathing right now.

Deep, slow, relaxing breaths that fill you with peace and calm, perhaps?

Mmmm.

Shallow breathing, when only your chest moves, is what we do when we are afraid and nervous; it stops oxygen from reaching the parts oxygen would love to visit and this makes us, you've guessed it, afraid and nervous. It's how most of us breathe all the time, even when we believe we're fine.

There are better ways to breathe that help our minds slow down, helping us to relax and feel more at home in our bodies.

Find a quiet place where you are unlikely to be disturbed.

Close your eyes and place your hands on your belly so that when you breathe, you can feel your belly rise.

Focus on a breath that comes in slowly through your nose and blows out of your mouth.

Do this twice more.

PS. Yawning is a good sign.

Try the breathing exercise whenever your mind starts to witter on and your brain's a-buzzing.

Three deep relaxing breaths to bring you some peace and quiet.

When you've got the hang of that, try breathing in as you think, 'I am calm', and as you exhale imagine that you're breathing out all those thoughts and stresses, just blow them away as far away as you can.

Breathe in calm, breathe out stress, breathe in calm...breathe in calm...breath in calm...

Some people like to do this for a bit longer, following their breath for say, ten minutes every day – the 'every day' bit is important because your mind and body get used to the routine and because ten minutes every day just has more benefit than a two hour battle with yourself every month or so.

It's meditation. To meditate means to ponder, explore, or focus on one thing, and when you meditate you're giving your mind something to do rather than letting it freestyle all over the place, which it loves to do.

If you want to try it, find a quiet place where you won't be disturbed for ten minutes, letting people know that you're busy for a while if necessary. Sit on a chair or on a cushion on the floor; just get comfy and find out what works for you.

Close your eyes and tell yourself now that you intend to sit quietly and don't want to be disturbed! Tell your mind that it can have ten minutes off and need not get involved – it may not take much notice at first, but with practice, it'll get the message!

Breathe deeply into your belly and exhale any tension or worry. Then just follow your breath as it comes into your nose, and follow it as it leaves. Just let the breath come and go – you don't need to change it, just go with it, observe it.

The trick is not to worry when you suddenly find yourself immersed in thoughts of dinner or football or why your little toe sticks out at a funny angle and you've no idea how you got onto that when you were meant to be focusing on your breathing, for pity's sake...When this happens, which it most certainly will, just take control of the reins again and get back to following that breath once more.

When your ten minutes is up (and you might want to place a watch nearby or set an alarm clock under a cushion so that it won't make you jump when it beeps) take your time opening your eyes and adjusting to the faster pace of the world around you. Stand up slowly and then stamp your feet to bring any energy that's in your head down to the ground and to prevent you feeling light-headed; having a drink of water and a snack can help too. You might feel more relaxed, more sensitive, more in control.

Let this feeling help to remind you to look after yourself once you get back out there again. Know that you can choose what thoughts and images make it back into your nice, calm mind, so choose well!

Scientists have proven that when we meditate, our brainwaves change from one state to another, and in this so-called Alpha state, our heart rate slows, we relax and all sorts of interesting things are possible.

If you like to know the whys and hows, why not do some research into the scientific background of the mediation phenomenon, and see what you can discover.

Then do your own practical research, be your own subject and meditate, and see what conclusions you come up with.

Remember that scientific proof is simply human beings' way of making sense of things. Human beings like to 'know' things; after all, it's interesting to explore how something works.

We 'know' now that the Earth orbits the Sun and not the other way round, it has been 'proved', but only fairly recently you might have got into a lot of trouble for suggesting something that seemed such a ridiculous notion. Just ask Galileo.

The Aboriginal people of Australia are said to have used telepathy to contact other people hundreds of miles away, which is quite a practical solution when you're trying to reach distant friends and there's nowhere to charge a mobile phone, let's face it.

Telepathy is the exchange of thoughts between people, and scientists in the west have recently done experiments proving that this is quite possible.

The people who live in the rainforest have used plants to heal themselves and their families for thousands of years; scientists from the western world are now discovering, after rigorous laboratory testing, that these plants do indeed contain certain chemicals and compounds that are now being used to create drugs routinely used in western medicine.

It seems that whilst two people from different times and places might use different words to describe their understanding of what something is or how something works, they may both be talking about the same thing. Western doctors with a headache might be really pleased that the chemical make-up of the rainforest willow tree can be used to make Aspirin tablets, whilst the indigenous medicine man or woman might thank the spirit of the tree for its healing power.

Worth remembering that proving something, however, is not the same as creating it or owning it or knowing it.

Everything exists before it is proven to exist, after all!

What do you think is out there that has yet to be proven? What have we yet to discover?

Allow yourself to wonder and think outside the normal way of things, right out into the Universe and beyond!

How do you think the world and our understanding of it might seem different in 10 years, 100 years or 1000 years? Let your imagination fill in the details!

Sometimes, because we have a name or an explanation for how something works, it can be tempting to think we 'know' it. We can file it away, tick it off and miss its true nature.

Challenge yourself to 'not know' something.

What is that ball of hot in the blue open that brings us light?

What is that wide wet that sometimes charges, sometimes glides through your city, depending on its mood?

Try looking beyond the words we give to things. Let your current understanding of something you think you know dissolve and look closely into it, feel as deeply into it as you can and just wonder! What's the furthest you can go into something? What do you find there?

Just have fun with this!

Like anything we do, whether it's riding a bike, learning a language, or making pancakes, things get easier and are more fun (and in the case of any dish that requires tossing into the air, can be a whole lot tastier) if we practise, and this also applies to meditation or to any of the little exercises found in this book. It applies to every little game you play, and it applies to the greatest game you'll ever play, that you're playing right now.

When we practise something, we discover which areas are rusty and in need of a little attention. By practising, going over the steps again and again from the beginning, we grow in confidence and are able to go deeper into the game, noticing aspects we might have missed before.

You know how sometimes you watch someone score a goal/play the piano/do a somersault and it's incredible and you stand there with your mouth open, full of admiration, and wonder, 'How do they make that look so easy?'

Well, that way of making something look effortless has taken ages, probably years of training, years of practising kick ups, spending hours a day doing scales or stretching exercises. This training means that when they come to the big match/ recital/gymnastic display, they just 'know' what to do without even thinking about it, in fact, if they were to think about what they were doing this would probably block the amazing flow they seem to have tapped into and they might stumble.

Playing the Game of Life can be like this. The daily practise of exercises like meditation, good breathing or creating time for stillness has real benefit and means that when you finish your ten minute exercise and come out into the world again, playing the game itself becomes easier and more enjoyable and those inevitable challenges that crop up now and again seem less daunting.

We can 'go with the flow', or tap into the stream of life and let it carry us, instead of spending a lot of effort wading up stream, forcing ourselves to move against the current.

This flow, this force we're talking about is the force that makes trees grow, the sky blue, the birds sing.

How do you feel about the possibility that there might be a force that knows what it's doing and is within all things, including you?

What is Nature? What makes it work?

Where does this kind of wondering lead you?

If it's nowhere, how does that feel? Where is 'nowhere'?!

If going with the flow *is* the natural way of things and there is this force that just *is*, and when you feel connected to this amazing force that some people might want to call Great Spirit, or God, or Goddess, or Allah or Tao or All That Is or anything else at all – (maybe it exists whether you call it anything or not!) – you may never want to feel any other way.

Connecting in to the flow of this Life Force happens when we forget who we think we are for a moment, like the genius footballer who just plays and feels 'in the zone'. It happens when we dare to open our hearts to the world, recognising that maybe there is something not just 'out there', but actually within us, that knows what is best for us at all times and in all situations, and it happens when you really dare to play the game.

Trees and birds and clouds don't get into the messes we do because they don't think thoughts like humans do – they just surrender to their treeness, or their birdiness or their (okay, you get the idea..!) and just *be*.

Human beings have been given this incredible gift of a mind that has the ability to create anything it focuses on, and because most of us simply aren't aware of the power we have to create our own world, we allow our minds to be spoon fed and manipulated by images dreamt up by others who aren't aware of their true nature either, so we spend a lot of our lives being distracted by the world we dream up, and by the limited image of ourselves we have created.

Maybe our natural state is one of peace and natural growth? Spend some time in nature, watching the birds, the animals, the river – when do you ever see a caterpillar worrying about how it looks to the other caterpillars and deciding not to go out today because it feels uptight? You don't!

And if You are part of nature, it might be that your natural way of being as a human being on this Earth is to allow Life to unfold through you, to let your true self emerge naturally. When we forget this and allow our minds to distract us, we can get a bit lost, things start to feel uncomfortable and we can feel like we're out of synch – and we are, we've lost our connection with what is natural, lost our rhythm. When we spend a little time listening out for, or listening into the rhythm again, it's like we pick up the beat, and can join the dance again.

There are people out there who are strong on the inside, confident and self-assured. They are relaxed and fun to be around.

How do they get to be this way?
Well, you now know the answer – they've just been practising!

Chapter 5

Time out

'Five minutes of today are worth as much to me as five minutes in the next millennium.
Let us be poised, and wise, and our own today.'
Ralph Waldo Emerson

What do the words 'Human Being' mean to you?
What does the word 'Being' mean to you?
What does it mean 'to be'?

You might look these words up in a dictionary, and see what another Human Being has thought before you, remembering that everything you ever read is just one person's viewpoint, and that yours is equally valid and worthwhile.

Follow your own instincts on this – and in all things, of course – and see what you come up with outside the dictionary definitions.

How much time do you spend being? Just Being?

When we allow ourselves 'to be' it means we are really in the Now, in the present moment. We're allowing ourselves to open up and let an experience happen through us, not worrying about what happened this morning or what might happen later on.

Funny things can happen when you're in this state, like time suddenly speeds up and when you look up from your painting or get off your bike or the music finishes, you might be amazed at how hours have flown by and yet it feels like only moments have passed.

29

To do something with all of you, to really give all your attention to where you are and what you are doing is how we experience things when we're really tiny, when everything is new, every sensation fresh and exciting.

We tend to lose this ability to experience life with such intensity as we grow older because we have clocks and you'd never get to school if you allowed yourself to be drawn in to every smell of every flower, or the feel of the grass between your toes because you'd taken off your shoes, or followed the song of the blackbird wherever it led you.

So it's important to get to school on time, but it is just as important to remember that experiencing the world as a child with our eyes fully open and the ability to be amazed by things we might have been taking for granted is a great way to play the game every now and then.

Try it and see for yourself.

Sometimes we can try to do so many things at once that we fail to give our full attention to any of them, like a juggler trying to keep a million balls in the air, or like the guy with the plates spinning on top of those pointy sticks. If we overstretch ourselves, things are likely to come crashing down on our heads and whilst that might be exciting and distracting for a while, maybe we might miss something important amidst the chaos.

A wise Chinese sage, Yun men, put it well when he suggested, *'In walking, just walk. In sitting, just sit. Above all, don't wobble.'* Which is excellent advice for plate spinners everywhere...

So when you find yourself eating a banana, finishing your coursework, wondering if s/he's going to call, worrying that your new haircut is a bit too weird, distracted by the scratchy bits down the back of your shirt, deciding to let it grow longer this time – and all this at once! - try taking a breath and remind yourself, 'I am here, now!' to bring yourself back into the moment and then choose one thing and one thing only to focus on!

Today, imagine you're doing something for the very first time.

Focus on really experiencing whatever it is you are doing as fully as you can.

When you eat your breakfast, just eat your breakfast. No talking, no TV, no last minute homework. Chew each mouthful and be aware of the food in your mouth, really taste it like you've never tasted toast before!

You might experience this kind of intensity when you walk, listen to music, have a bath.

Allow yourself to really experience what walking is, what listening is, what a bath is. Allow your senses to show you all they can, all that is possible if your attention is focused on just being in the now.

You might also try spending some time on your own with no distractions. That means no TV, no music, no food or other people. Aim to sit quietly or lie down for ten minutes (without going to sleep, as that would be another way to avoid being still) and just BE. Yep, be a human being for a while, not a human doing!

Listen to the sounds in the quiet – you might find it's the noisiest silence you've ever heard – and just breathe. If you find yourself becoming uncomfortable or twitchy, gently ask yourself why you're feeling that way; maybe you've been avoiding thinking about or feeling something and this is the time that you're trying to get your own attention. Certain emotions might begin to come to the surface because you've created some space – just allow yourself to feel them fully and then let them go. Whatever happens is fine – there's no one there to see you and this is a real gift to yourself.

Know that each time you do this or the meditation exercise, it will be different, because each time you do it, *you* are different.

Any athlete knows that in order to perform or play at their very best, there are times to move and stretch and exercise, but equally important is the time they spend resting. This isn't being lazy. It's vital to make time to allow their body and mind to rest and absorb what they've been through in order to be stronger and fitter next time.

It's like when you dance – you can feel that the times that your body is still, even for a moment, are just as important to the dancing as the moving and wiggling and shimmying about, as if what *isn't* done allows us to see or feel what *is* done more clearly.

Apply this to music, football, painting, gardening, swimming, having a conversation with a friend – anything! Unless there is space to pause, all you'd have is a mess of stuff crammed in together – hideous noise instead of music; everyone running at the ball with no one to pass to in football; both of you chattering at once instead of taking turns to talk and to listen.

The same idea applies to all of us playing this amazing Game of Life – times of quiet and stillness and rest are absolutely vital to enjoying and playing our game at our best, making the times of action more energised, focused and fun.

Just as a car can only travel for so many miles without needing to stop and refuel, or a fire last so long before needing more wood to feed it, so as human beings taking responsibility for ourselves and really beginning to Live as if we are truly alive, we know that to do and do and do and do and do would exhaust us, not only physically, but emotionally, mentally and spiritually too.

To push yourself, not to listen to the signs that you need rest is to risk blowing a fuse or burning out and being forced, in a really extreme way, to stop.

Spend at least 5 minutes everyday giving yourself some time out, alone and in stillness.

Before you go to sleep at night is a good time to really allow yourself to relax completely. Often, we can fall asleep still knotted up with all the day's tension only to wake up with a sore neck, or our minds are on automatic and we can't seem to get them to switch off. Try this...

Before getting into bed, give your duvet a good shake (remembering to clear anything that's been dumped on it first, or you'll have books and socks and custard creams you've forgotten about flying across the room...)

Plump up your pillow and make your bed a welcoming, cosy place that you want to get into.

Lying down, just allow yourself to sink into the sheets. Take three of those magic breaths and imagine yourself letting go of the day, knowing that you've done all you can and that if you need to, you can pick up where you left off tomorrow.

You might want to imagine yourself just popping out to a recycling lorry parked handily outside and handing over any worries or anxieties – see them in your mind's eye, tip them all in and see the lorry drive away, taking them off to be transformed into something more useful, like an answer

---

to a problem, that will be delivered to you in time for your day tomorrow.

Think of something that was positive about your day – maybe someone smiled at you on the bus; you noticed new little green leaves coming on the oak tree just past your house; maybe you just got through it and that is enough. Smile to yourself and say 'Thanks!' for these things. Saying Thank You has a way of opening our hearts to something bigger than ourselves and so connects us to that amazing natural energy – some might call it Love, baby – that flows through all things. Gratitude is a fab attitude to cultivate in yourself!

Get ready now to go through each part of your body, first tensing it for a few seconds and then relaxing it.

Start by wiggling your toes and feet. Feel how it is to move them, then relax, stop moving and experience how this feels. Then tense the muscles in your legs for a few seconds – start by lifting the left leg a few inches off the bed, then do the same on the right side – and then let go.

Move on up through your body: Squeeze your butt and then relax. Tense the muscles in your torso and back by gently lifting your head up and off the pillow as if you were starting to sit up, then lie back and relax completely.

Clench your left hand for a few seconds, and then allow it to open, and follow with your right.

Lift your left and right arms up a few inches off the bed, and then allow them to fall gently.

Move up to your head and screw up your whole face,

clenching your jaw and wiggling your ears if you are blessed in this way! Now completely let go.

You have felt the experience of tension and how that feels in your body, and you have experienced how it feels to relax. Allow yourself to breath deeply, breathing in relaxation, and breathing out relaxation, at your own pace. Listen to your body and if you sense any places that feel sore or stuck, just imagine a warm energy flowing to that place and soothing it.

Allow yourself to let go and just be in this feeling of peace, breathing slowly. Allow yourself to fall into sleep.

Night!

Chapter 6

Check In, Check Out...

'We have all a better guide in ourselves, if we would attend to it, than any other person can be.'
Jane Austen

So your mind is deep black velvet sprinkled with stars, you live in a minimalist paradise and all you're left with is this great big scary silence that doesn't help at all. Fantastic.

Hold on.

This is a bit of a special silence, and it gives you time, room and space to take a deep breath (or three) and listen for something. Shhhh. Listen.

And this might sound bizarre, but you are listening for what the *real* you, the heart of you, what the very core of you, my little orange pippin you, has to say on the matter.

You're listening to the part of you that would speak if only you were brave and fantastic and creative, gorgeous and witty enough.

Right. If only.

Well – listen to this – you are!

Yep, I know it's a bit hard to hear anything with all that other racket going on, but when all the doubtingnegativechatteringboringheavystuff shuts up, it's what you're left with.

Your true voice.

It's like the bestest best friend in the universe. It'll only ever tell you the truth, it'll only recommend things that support you and it'll be dead pleased you've finally realised it's there after all this time.

Really?

Really.

Cor.

Exciting stuff.

Of course, sometimes you might choose to completely ignore what it has to say.

Remember this..?

Tired and Worried You Ok, I know I'll feel sick if I even touch that last slab of chocolate cake, but I really am enjoying it.

True You No, you're not. You're feeling depressed because...

Tired and Worried You Pardon? Did somebody speak?

True You Take a walk. Dance round the room. Make a list of some of the good things that happened today...

Tired and Worried You Sniff. Cake. I want it. Think I'll stick the TV on too.

Even More Tired You (later) Yuk. I feel sick. That was rubbish. I'm knackered.

And have you sorted out the real problem? Nope. Just avoided it, and now you're all tangled up in a tired sugar-fuelled TV daze. You can just about fall into bed, where you wake up even more tired than when you fell asleep, and you still feel bad about whatever started all this off in the first place.

We've all been there.

But the cool thing is that your True Voice never sneers, 'I told you so…'

Nope. It knows you feel bad enough as it is, and that you need all the energy you can muster up to bring yourself back to a place where you can see clearly and feel strong enough to face the next bit.

Ask it later, 'But why did I do/say/think that?' and it'll help you see why.

And if that isn't bestbuddy enough for you, it's there to help you choose your next move.

It helps you feel good about yourself because it is your self. Your true self.

Conjure up a dream buddy who would be with you whenever you needed them. Describe this new best friend in detail. How would you feel when you were around them?

Imagine that they are with you next time you feel in need of a bit of support – what would they say to you? Does their advice help?

Know that this kind of support is available to you every moment, and that you just have to give yourself the space and the time to listen, and make friends with yourself!

The first step to being able to hear what your true self has to say on the matter is to start listening to all those little signs and signals that your body gives you throughout the day. Simply put, your tummy rumbles, you reach for a banana; you yawn and can't keep your eyes open, you go to sleep. If your head starts to ache and you've been staring at the computer for hours, it's a good bet that you need a rest; if you've been doing your homework for so long you can't remember your own name, let alone the finer strategic points of the Battle of Bosworth Field, and your arms and legs feel all jittery, then again, it's a clear signal that you need to shake some of that heady stuff out and move your body.

By listening to, and then, most importantly, acting on these signals we are able to keep balanced despite all the odd things we like to do during the course of an average day.
It's important that our body knows that we're listening and taking it seriously, because we all know how it feels to be ignored.

Just look at the little boy in the supermarket trying to get his dad's attention: dad's wrestling with the frozen foods and trying to stuff them into one of those silly plastic bags[*] that splits and, oops! jettisons produce all over the shocked cashier (shocked, because dad didn't really say oops! at all, let's face it) and meanwhile, the little boy has been waiting patiently for dad to acknowledge his need for the most enormous bar of chocolate he's ever seen in his life, placed handily just at his eye level. When dad seems to be unaware of his polite requests, a steady whine begins and then the stamping follows, there are tears and screaming and it is horrible.

So beware – ignore the signals your body is sending you and you too could be lying on the floor with your legs in the air surrounded by embarrassed onlookers and get sent to bed later without any pudding...

Or put it this way, if we choose to ignore our body's excellent advice, you can guarantee it will find a way to get you to listen by

---

* Plastic bags just aren't good for anyone or anything, and their use can lead to all sorts of calamity and chaos, as this example shows. Far better to have some handy cotton bags stuffed into your pockets to use whenever you go shopping, don't you think, dad?

being more vigorous in its approach, which is when we get ill. Illness, or dis-ease (see that? Great, aren't they, words?) is the last resort of the system (made up of your body, your mind and emotions and the shiny spirit bit of you) that is trying to help you at all times to feel good in your own skin and to enjoy this amazing game we're all playing.

So, next time you're in the supermarket/lunch queue/fridge, ask yourself, (and that's your True Self, by the way) what's best for you to eat. Follow your own advice, and see how you feel.
Start small like this, pay attention, and you'll begin to recognise the signs and signals, what they mean and so begin applying this method of checking in with yourself out in the big, wide world that is your life.

And if you need the truth, or you need to make a really important decision? You need to hear what your True Voice has to say on the matter...

First, find a space where you can be quiet and alone, if possible. The less distraction the better.
Then, go through the breathing exercise you know, with your hands placed on your belly, breathing in slowly through your nose and then out through your mouth. Feel yourself slowing down, relaxing and letting go of everything you don't need for this short time; know that you can pick up where you left off afterwards, but for now, all you need is this moment.

When you feel calm and centred in your body, move your hands up to your heart and place them there. This is the place that knows what is best for you in all situations and at

---

all times. Allow yourself to smile and send some of that warm, smiley feeling down to your heart. Now ask whatever it is that you need to ask. You might start with a yes/no type of question, to get used to the feelings you get and what they mean.

Is X a healthy person for me to be around? Is physics a good choice for me to make this year?

You'll know if your true self is sending you the message that, 'Yes! This is a positive move' because you'll feel a warmth, like a gorgeous glow that makes you want to smile. At the other end of the scale, 'This is absolutely not in your best interest' will feel very different, perhaps like a caving in, an emptiness, or just plain wrong.

Remember, this is just a guide, and how it feels exactly will vary from person to person, and what it takes is practice at tuning in to your own feelings.
Some people will feel things in different parts of their body – some people might get an all over whoosh! of energy or tingly hands if something is right; others might feel an uncomfortable feeling in their belly that indicates something not so healthy. Some people may 'see' something in their mind's eye; others will get a hunch, they'll 'just know' when something is right or not.

Experiment.

By tuning in to the signals that your body is sending you, you'll be able to make choices that empower you, based on something far more substantial than the pressure exerted on you by a million different sources that do not necessarily have your best interests at heart. And when you follow your intuition (the way you just 'know' something, but you're not sure how), which is a very real sense that we all possess although not all of us are aware of it, Life suddenly becomes a lot more fun and though it may sound odd at first, start to make a lot more sense!

Albert Einstein once said, 'The only real, valuable thing is intuition.' And as well as having the coolest hair on the planet, he did know quite a lot of good stuff.

Keep an intuition diary this week. If you get a hunch about something, or you make a guess that is proved right, make a note of it. Start to become aware of how in tune with things you really are. And if you make a guess and it doesn't turn out how you expected, don't worry about it – stay open to the possibility that your next one might turn out right.

Intuition is a sense that improves with use, so by exercising it, our sense gets sharper.

Most of all, keep it fun!

Chapter 7

Branching Out

'God bless the roots! Body and soul are one!'
Theodore Roethke

Congratulations! Your number has come up and you have been given a brand new car! You lucky thing!

What's more, you can choose any model you want. So, what's it to be? Sleek, red Porsche with leather seats? Might not be everyone's choice that, believe it or not, so how about a cute, nippy Mini with sunroof and fantastic stereo? You fancy something a little less showy, that doesn't go that well but something you can tinker with and love into life? It's yours!!

> What would you choose? Describe the vehicle of your dreams in the finest possible detail.
>
> Look it over in your imagination and change the furry dice from red to green if that's what you want.
>
> Anything goes (unless the engine needs a bit of work, and that might be just the challenge you're ready for...).

Weyhay! So, here it is!

It's beautiful, whatever the neighbours think, and it's all yours. You're the registered keeper, the one who's responsible for looking after the little beauty.

You take some time to walk round it a few times, just breathing in its fantastickness, proudly shining the paintwork with your sleeve, just placing your hand on the bonnet and feeling good.

You're full of good intentions, of course you are. Going to keep it clean and shiny and smelling great, use the fuel best suited to its engine and take it out regularly to keep it happy.

Even if it starts out a bit messy and run down, it soon begins to feel comfortable and is a great place to sit and travel to far off places, if only in your imagination at first.

You love it, and it loves you back.

And all those years ago, (and bet you can guess which twisty turny road this one's heading down...) when you finally reached destination Planet Earth, you needed a vehicle to get around in; not so much a little runabout at first as a little lie-about-sleeping-and-burping-mobile. As your needs changed, this amazing machine did too. It had been designed with you specifically in mind and so adapted moment by moment to the circumstances in which you found yourself.

This amazing machine is your body. And not just any old body, either.

It climbs trees and it mends the cuts and the bruises. It dances and stretches, it might do cartwheels in the park. It protects you from the rain, and it shivers and sneezes to remind you to wear a coat next time.

Look at your hands. They are beautiful. Through them you contact your world. You might speak with your hands, and they certainly have as many moods as you do: feel nervous, they'll be twitching; you're energised and they're flying around like birds in a wide sky; angry and find them balled into fists ready to explode...

Put on your favourite music and with every click of your fingers list all the things your hands do for you.

Do actually know your body? I mean, really know it?
Can you point to where your liver lives? How about your
spleen? Your kidneys?
Make it your mission to locate the organs in your body and
find out what they do for you.

It's surprising how good this can make you feel. It's like the satis-
fying feeling you get when you learn how to wire a plug, or a
seed you planted starts to grow, or you mend your little brother's
bike. You feel more involved and part of something. Your body is
where you live, after all. You might as well do some looking
around and get to know the place.

Take off your socks and say hello to your feet. If you're
lucky, they carry you everywhere you want to go. Give
them a rub, recognising that they've been with you since
you were born and have put up with a lot. Say Thank You,
Feet! and feel them wiggle to be appreciated.

Close your eyes and smile to each part of your body – a real
and loving smile – and say thank you for the amazing job it
does for you without you even having to ask.
Don't be surprised if your body has a few things to say to
you too, if you listen!

So you look after your vehicle and it's all good. However, you put
plums in the petrol tank of your new car, and what happens? (My
little brother is well aware of the consequences of this behaviour
– being grounded for forever is one of them...)
The car won't start, it makes strange groaning noises and is

obviously a bit upset. It refuses to run at all until the plums are out of its system and its tank is full, once again, with the good quality fuel it needs to enjoy doing its job well.

Plums? Petrol tanks? Particular relevance to anything in the known universe?

Well, eat rubbish and you'll feel rubbish, it's obvious, and there are people everywhere testing out the finer points of this theory for themselves at every mealtime.

Our bodies are pretty amazing places to live in and they tell us stuff all the time, and it's interesting to start listening say, after you drink fizzy water mixed with caffeine, sugar, colourings and flavourings. The amazing rush you feel is followed by an exhausted slump that makes you reach for another fizzy water mixed with caffeine, sugar, colourings and flavourings (someone should really think up a catchy name for this evil concoction...) just to get you going again. Yum.

Do you think maybe, just maybe, the monster headache you get when the effects wear off and that is only eased by having another one might be trying to say something along the lines of, 'Um, mine's an apple juice next time, please'?

It's easy when we listen to our bodies. Eating up our veggies and drinking good water makes our body a comfortable, happy place for us to live.

But it's also really easy to ignore the very clear messages our body is sending us. We might say that we never really realised they could communicate. Sometimes our heads are so full of chatter that we forget we've got a body at all. And sometimes we hear the messages, ignore them and eat rubbish because the taste of that stuff makes us feel better. For about ten seconds, at least.

Your body knows what it wants and what it needs for optimum performance.
It will choose food that is as close to its original state or as alive as possible because it knows that the more something has been refined and processed, the longer it has been picked from the Earth and left waiting on a shelf, the further away it is from the healthy food it used to be.

The more relaxed you are, the closer you feel to the ground, the more likely you are to make healthy, life-supporting choices. And this applies, not just to those times you find yourself ravenous in the kitchen, but to every area of your life.

Now let's move on from plums and petrol tanks. We're going to do something far more sensible. We're going to stand like a tree. And before our minds kick in and scream, 'This is ridiculous!!!' (Ah, too late..?), we'd better get on with it...

Trees are incredible and do such amazing things on this planet, taking in the carbon dioxide and recycling it into the oxygen we human beings need to survive here, for one.

If you can visit a tree near you, that's great, otherwise make your way to anywhere outside where you won't be disturbed; even if you're stuck indoors, you can bring to mind a beautiful place you know and imagine yourself there.

Find a good spot and stamp your feet and feel any energy stuck in your head or anywhere else in your body moving down into the Earth.

Stand with your feet shoulder width apart and imagine that your legs are planted deep into the Earth, so that you are solidly supported. Try not to stick your bottom out as your arms hang naturally loose by your sides, and imagine that your spine, your amazingly flexible trunk, is being gently pulled up to the sky.

Now take your mind down and imagine that, just like a tree, you are receiving energy from the Earth through your fantastic rooty feet.

Breathe in good, fresh air and breathe out old thoughts, worries and stale energy to be recycled into energy that is more healthy and life-giving. You might want to shut your eyes as you start to feel the energy circulating round your body and reaching the very tips of your fingers, the tip of your nose.

And just stand as a tree stands, wise and strong and flexible, for a while.

When you're ready, gently wiggle your fingers, your toes, opening your eyes and becoming aware of the sounds and sights around you. Take your time. Slowly stretch and move your whole body until you're ready to return home. Say Thanks! to the tree and the place you've spent this time in.

Then, obviously, you make like a tree, and leave.

This exercise is useful because it brings us fully into our physical body, helping us to feel more grounded and rooted, and so able to make decisions from a more focused place. When we are in this place, we are also more able to hear what the quiet voice of our intuition has to say.

So, next time you feel yourself reaching for the shiny pretend food (read the ingredients list, and discover what is really lying in the fridge masquerading as a sausage roll...), ask your body what it wants. It knows. And be prepared for your head chatter to interrupt just as your body is about to make a suggestion, and be prepared for the chatter to make an extremely persuasive case for the genetically modified sweety snack. At this point, take the three breaths, thank your chatter for its input, and listen again to what your body has to say.

You might be surprised when it tells you that you're not actually hungry at all, but avoiding doing your history project. Or that you want the sweety snack because you're feeling a bit down and sweet things are comforting because they remind us of being small and looked after and soothed by a sweet like when we fell off the big slide that time in the park. Or that you're feeling a bit odd because it's one o'clock in the afternoon and you haven't had anything to eat for breakfast and as a consequence your blood sugar is on the floor, looking up at you and quietly but firmly putting in an order for toast and juice tomorrow morning, please.

Then again, your body might think that rice and veggies sounds like just the thing to keep a body going through the day. Enjoy!

And this is absolutely not about becoming fussy or paranoid about what you eat. It's about becoming aware and making choices that support you from moment to moment. Some moments might be longer and more challenging than others, so lunch had better be tasty and energising.

Choose a country, find out about its traditional cuisine and prepare a meal for your family and friends some time this week.

Play some traditional music, maybe learn a word or two in a new language, dress differently. Maybe ask all your guests to bring along something associated with your chosen place.

Eat well and have fun!

Chapter 8

Pushing the Boundaries

'Invent your world. Surround yourself with people, colour, sounds and work that nourish your soul.'
Sark

Energy. Absolutely everything is made up of this amazing stuff, vibrating at differing speeds. Me, you, the fridge, a star. The slower it vibrates, the denser and heavier something is; the faster it goes, the lighter and more refined it is. Sometimes it's so fine we can't see it, but that doesn't mean it doesn't exist.

> Try this experiment...Give your hands a good shake and then rub them together as if you were making a plasticine worm between them until they feel really warm. Then, really slowly, palms facing each other, move them apart a few inches. Move them together again, then slowly apart a little further this time.
> Do this a couple of times. What can you feel?

The squishy, warm feeling, like you've got a rubber ball between your hands, is you detecting the sensation of your own energy. If you run your finger along your arm right now, you know that that's you, you can feel it and see it. However, if you run your finger an inch or two away from the edge of your arm, it's still you. In fact, your energy, or energy field, extends out for a few feet - the healthier and more energised you are, the further out it goes!

We all know how it feels if someone stands just that bit too close to us – that squirmy uncomfortable feeling happens because they are standing in our energy space, and if their energy isn't in tune with ours, it feels strange. And just as we brush our teeth and have a wash at the end of the day to feel refreshed and clean, so it's important to make sure that our energy field is sparkly too. Yep - our energy field is a bit like a fishing net that collects all sorts of bits and pieces over the course of an average day. If you don't give it a good shake every now and then, just imagine how heavy, not to mention stinky, it's going to get. Some people are walking round with years' worth, a lifetime's worth of energetic debris hanging about all around them in a soupy, dusty, yucky old cloud. Wonder how that feels?

Take three deep breaths into your belly and feel how strong you are at your centre.

Now, rub your hands together till they're warm and then, with your hands about six inches away from your body, literally brush yourself all over, from head to toe.

Imagine all the bits and pieces being cleared away and polish your energy field up till it's shiny.

Finish off by imagining yourself stood under a waterfall of light that pours over you, cleansing any areas you might have missed and generally making you feel absolutely fantastic!

You know how some people are so nice to be around, how being around them just makes you feel good, and you're not sure why? And you know how it can be around certain people who make you feel a bit uncomfortable, even make your skin crawl, and you don't know why? It's their energy interacting with yours, and if it doesn't feel good, you've some choices to make.

See, energy isn't a solid thing, it likes to flow and mix, like paints when you spill them onto white paper; sometimes the colours mix and it looks beautiful, but other times you might end up with a dark, sludgy mess. When two people interact, there is always an energy exchange going on, and so if you hang out with a certain person and always end up feeling drained and depressed at the end of the night, whereas they seem to be enjoying the whole thing, then you can be pretty sure that your energy is being affected by theirs. Just being aware of this rather nifty phenomenon is useful as it empowers you to choose who you hang out with.

(Sometimes it's tricky to remove yourself from a draining situation, but the energy shield exercise that is coming up later is perfect for those times.)

So, as well as brushing your teeth and having a wash, it's important to give your energy field (some people call it an aura) a good brush down at the end of the day, or whenever you feel a bit mixed up.

It's especially important if you've been around an argument, or been upset or felt any strong emotions – emotions are real things, they're swirling clouds of energy, and unless the emotion is cleared and dispersed or transformed into a more positive emotion, it will settle in your energy field and you'll be carrying it round with you.

Ever felt like you couldn't shake off a mood? This is why.

Energy might take on different colours or flavours, but it's always just energy at its centre. As it can never be created or destroyed, it just changes from one state to another, which is about the only thing I can really remember from my physics lessons (that and a particularly bizarre lesson when the ticker tape experiments got out of hand and the room ended up full to the ceiling with

53

streams of paper, all of us taking full advantage of the situation to get as excited and silly as possible, like little kids in a snowstorm...Our teacher floundering upon a sea of paper ribbons, calling weakly for us to, yep, you've guessed it, simmer down. Frankly, he had no chance...).

So what do we do then if we find ourselves in a situation that feels bad? The argument going on at the bus stop has nothing to do with you, but somehow, even after you've arrived at your stop and walked away, you can't forget it and you feel a bit jumpy for a while.

If everything is energy, then it's possible to feel the anger and confusion of a situation as clearly as if a bucket of the stuff has been thrown all over you. Even if you can't actually see it, it's there, and you've been soaked through. Taking out your brolly at the right time to deflect the deluge means it won't get to you, but just bounce right off.

Remember that phrase, 'Sticks and stones may break my bones, but words can never hurt me'? Just not true! Just because we can't hold a word in our hands doesn't mean it can't hurt us like a knife. Words, like a sneer or a look that takes a second, are extremely powerful, if we allow them to be. And that is the magic bit – it's up to us to protect ourselves from all that negative stuff that's flying about all over the place.

The world is full of amazingcreativefantasticfun stuff, it's true, but a moment spent watching the news or outside in the playground when you're five years old is proof enough that the world can also be frighteningdangerousconfusinguncertain and the more responsibility we take for our own lives, the more fun we can have and the more useful we can be in the world.

Knowing how to protect ourselves in certain situations is an essential part of Playing the Game to its fullest. It prevents us getting swept along by other people's moods and agendas; it enables us to keep our feet on the ground and make choices based on how we truly feel inside; it keeps us connected with our own true power, which makes us stronger and safer and more confident.

Having an argument, or just being around negative moods, can feel physically bad. We might feel a tightness in our belly or our heart – ever seen someone fold their arms across the front of their body, hunching their shoulders and turning their body away from the source of negative energy? If this happens to you and you can't leave right away, remember to breathe deep warm breaths into the area that feels sore or tight to stop feelings getting stuck, and imagine the stuckness melting away.

One of the easiest ways to protect ourselves is to choose to walk away from a situation that feels unhealthy. You don't need to make the others involved feel bad, but a simple, 'I've got to go now' does the trick simply and quickly.

Sometimes, leaving just isn't possible and another form of protection is required. Some people's preferred way of protecting themselves is to hide. Very sensible, as long as you remember to come out of the burrow when the danger has passed. Others prefer to use anger, or rudeness or being cute or clever to hide how they're feeling inside. Only problem is, with all these forms of boundary between ourselves and whatever is threatening us, we risk losing ourselves somewhere in there; we're not being true to ourselves when we behave in that way.

We all wear a bit of armour to protect ourselves now and again, and it's only sensible to wear protective clothing in the midst of all those hazardous situations that Life seems to throw at us. Only, what started off as a breast plate here and one of those silvery helmets with the visor thingy there can escalate until you're lugging round the full Arthurian Knight get up, just to pop to the shop to get the paper for your dad. Feeling a bit weighed down, it's not surprising that you're not really noticing what's going on around you, that the old man standing on the corner is having trouble bending down to pick up the change he's dropped, and a little girl with the most fantastic beamy smile aimed at you has just skipped past and...

You get the idea that wearing all this stuff, (and especially shuffling along in those ridiculous pointy metal shoes...) means you might not be as sensitive or see things as clearly as you might.

There's a difference between protecting yourself sensibly and never opening up to anything new ever again. And as we've seen, sporting full armour at all times is a trifle wearing. People look at you funny and besides, the chafing is terrible...But never fear, there are better ways to protect yourself in situations where you feel threatened.

The best way is to create an energy shield around yourself. Yep, a magic invisible shield that lets in all the healthy, positive stuff and filters out the rest, bouncing any negative stuff coming your way right off. And before you roll your eyes, saying, 'Yeah, right. This is like something out of Harry Potter...' just try it. It works. Like all the ideas in this book, it's in here because it's simple and it really works.

Before you leave the house in the morning, stand still, stamp your feet and take some deep breaths with your eyes closed, blowing away any tension and worries. Now, with your next out breath, slowly push out your hands as if you're pushing away something heavy in front of you. Then push out to the sides and above your head, breathing out a strong breath each time you push.

Imagine an egg-shaped shield all around you extending as far as your hands can go, glowing silvery white, or blue, or gold, or whatever feels a good, safe, strong colour to you. Imagine it glowing really brightly around you.

Now take a final deep breath into your belly, and place your hands over your navel and give your tummy a rub so you feel completely strong and centred in your body.

Open your eyes, smile and go forth, proud warrior, into your day.

If you find yourself in an unhealthy or uncomfortable situation, remember that your shield is shining and protecting you.
You might want to imagine anything negative coming your way just bouncing off, or even, (as this shield is the super duper deluxe version, of course) being transformed into something a bit nicer. Stars. Bluebirds. Jelly beans. That bit's up to you.

Note: To maintain the qualities of your shield and promote long life and overall effectiveness, we suggest cleaning your shield at the end of every day or whenever it's had a battering, whichever is sooner. To do this, rub your hands together briskly until they are warm and proceed to shine and rub all over the surface of your shield, brushing away anything that may have got stuck there. Energetic chewing gum may take several attempts to remove, but persevere until your shield is shiny and clear. In this way, your shield will last your lifetime. We trust you will enjoy both.

Chapter 9

Who Am I, Anyway?

'We are what we think. With our thoughts we make the world.'
Buddha

I am I am I am happy worried silly afraid of rain barbed wire doing nothing I am a joker pigeon-fancier ace poker player dancer I am mad at things good at growing things rubbish at remembering things I am nothing really lost so full of joy I want to jump up and touch those high branches and so I do I am down I am up up and down I have brown hair hair that sticks up all over the place red hair, no, that was yesterday, it's blue now blue eyes brown *green* one brown one blue my skin is freckle-speckled the colour of polished wood I have a scar on my right cheek, see it? my feet are beautiful my feet are so ugly yuk stinky I love my solid feet I am a brother sister daughter son aunty uncle cousin friend *grannie's sweetiepop* I am fifteen eighteen twelve fourteen tomorrow looking forward to dinner having my ears pierced getting out of here I love pickled onions trees red sky at night the blackcurrant ones cars swimming in the lake hot chocolate...

We are all so different.

Who am I, anyway?
I am...I am handing over to you now to write/sing/whisper/dance/paint/sculpt your own unique answer to this question.
Use phrases like 'I have...' 'I wonder about...' 'I love...' to start you off.
If you come to a halt, just repeat the phrase 'I am... I am... I am... I am going to keep on doing this until something comes to me...'

And when you're done, take a moment to consider what an interesting, fascinating, complex being you really are. Yep, you truly are a bit special!

What is your name?
Do you know where it comes from, what it means, why your parents chose it for you? Do a little research into this word that has been with you for so long.
Find out what stories might be associated with this name.
Do they mean anything to you and your life now?

Now imagine yourself without a name.
Who are you now?
You might like to repeat the 'I am I am...' exercise that started this chapter, and see if any new insights into yourself, without the name that everyone calls you, come up.
Explore what you might be, what you are.

Some people around the world change their names over the course of their lifetime to mark the changes and times of growth in their lives. Think back to a time that changed you in some way – maybe you were hurt but grew stronger from the experience, or you set out to achieve something and reached your goal – what names would have been appropriate for you at those times?

Maybe the name of an animal, a star, or a river to reflect the qualities you displayed?

If you were to choose your own name right now, at this time in your life, what would you choose to reflect who and what you are?

And as She Who Asks Many Questions To Reach The Truth (and make your head spin as an interesting side effect..!) I ask you, if you were to close your eyes and search deep deep deep in your heart for your True Name, what would you find?
What is your True Name?

Listen, be open and see what comes to you – maybe words, pictures or a single symbol. Explore the meanings they may have for you, and enjoy!

No one else has quite that unique mix of talents/character-istics/challenges that you do, and it might be that some of the stuff that is part of you feels a bit heavy and difficult, but there are ways to deal with it and transform it into something useful if that's what you want to do.

You know, compost (stay with me here...) might start off as all the bits no one wants any more, chucked into the bin, but it trans-forms into something really useful that feeds new life and those sunflowers growing in the bottom of your garden are all nodding their heads in golden agreement to this rather ridiculously flowery way of putting things!

> There are no sunflowers growing in the bottom of your garden? Then why not plant a seed, look after it and watch it grow?
>
> You have no garden? A window box or a pot will do.

If you really want to do something, you can always find a way, and the start of anything new begins as a seed inside someone's head. It's up to us whether or not we nurture that seedy idea until it becomes something real out there in the world.

Remember the go-cart/victoria sponge/mother's day card you made that started its life as an idea sparked off by looking at your baby brother's pram in a new light/going to the bakers and thinking, 'I can do that!'/your Reception teacher giving you a tube of glitter, some yellow card and a space on the craft table..?

> Remember something positive you have created. Trace its origins right back.
>
> What prompted you to have the idea and how did you go about making it happen?
>
> How did you feel when you looked then at what you had made?

So if we can create something positive by just thinking about it and then acting out those thoughts, it follows that it's also possible to create stuff that might not be so good for us. Heavens, it seems that we're kind of creating our lives every minute just by the thoughts we're thinking. Think you're rubbish and your life will soon feel full of it. Guaranteed. So, quick. We'd better start doing something positive right now...

Think of a time when you felt really, really good, for a really, really good reason. Maybe you helped someone out, or you found a starfish on the beach when you were five or someone noticed how great you are and told you so...

Get that warm, fizzy, fuzzy feeling going, and see if you can make it grow, right to the ends of your fingers, try to make your hair stand on end with it. Cool!

Now imagine that feeling making its way out into the space all around you and further out even than that, expanding out to fill the room, the house, the street, the country, the universe!

Imagine that everything there is absorbing some of those good vibes and feeling a little better, thanks to you. Enjoy this for a while.

When you're ready, just bring your focus back down to you and into your own heart and feel good, just for you. Then, place both hands on your belly, your centre, and focus your attention there with a few deep breaths until you're ready to open your eyes.

This is good to do at any time, when you get up in the morning or whilst sitting at the bus stop. It only takes a minute and can really enable you to feel more focused and positive. Remember too that the energy we give out is what we are going to get back, so you might as well choose to have some good feelings coming your way.

If you find yourself thinking anything negative about anything at all, choose to replace it with some thought that makes you feel good. A thought of a beautiful place, your favourite baby cousin, the time you did something to help out the older lady next door – anything that will start the smiley, warm feeling you get inside when you feel good.

Add this to your collection of good things to do that make you feel better, healthy little habits to get you back on your path and feeling better at any time. These are usually short little exercises or games that slow down your mind and focus your energy in your body so you feel more centred and real and 'Ah yes! Here I am again!'

Choose the ones that work best for you and stick with them, then your mind knows what to do after a few tries and doesn't panic or get flustered, worrying if it's doing them 'right' or not. A flustered mind can lead to all sorts of mayhem, so next time you find yourself in a panic, take those three deep breaths and gently, but firmly, tell your mind that it is time to calm down, to let go of the situation and rest for a moment, for the good of all. This really works!

Sometimes our minds need to know that, whilst they are amazing, they don't know everything and cannot sort out everything at once. This might be a bit scary for your mind to hear, but reassure it, remind it to rest, and then breathe!

We all need reminding to look at things positively every now and again, so I'll hand over to Picasso for the last word on this:

'Do you know what you are? You are a marvel. You are unique. In all the

years that have passed, there has never been another like you. Your legs, your arms, your clever fingers, the way you move. You have the capacity for anything...Yes, you are a marvel.'

Gracias, Pablo!

Chapter 10

The Sand in your Sandwiches bit...

'I learned that courage was not the absence of fear, but the triumph over it.
The brave man is not he who does not feel afraid, but he who conquers that fear.'
Nelson Mandela

Dum dee dum dum dum...so there you are, wandering along, feeling pretty good about things. Life feels ok/more than ok/pretty cool when suddenly a horrible, mean little voice sneers, 'Oh yeah? And who do you think you are?'

What?

'What d'you think you're doing? Thinking you're so clever, so cool. Yeah right.'

Um.

'No one wants to read this. Why bother? Might as well stop writing right now. Turn on the TV. Have a biscuit. There. That's better.'

ENOUGH!

Before this little exchange goes any further, before the words stop here and this book-writing thing remains just a dream, let's see what's going on. Just who is this manipulative profferer of sugary snacks?

Well, have you ever been about to try something new (snowboarding/ lasagne/ talking to the girl at the bus stop), when

suddenly a little voice pipes up, 'Ahem! Hold on a minute.'
You stop (waxing your board/ fork raised/ mouth open, about to speak).

The voice continues, 'Why do you want to do that? You'll only look like an idiot/ You'll hate it anyway/ You'll get absolutely nowhere. Trust me.'

Now you really stop. 'Yeah, but I want to. It'll be...'

'...a disaster. I wouldn't bother.'

'But...'

And then they really get nasty. Let's treat ourselves to some of the old favourites.

'You! But you always mess up. What an idiot. You're rubbish at this sort of thing. Everyone'll laugh...'

And this could go on, and on. But no more. Nope. Enough.

Well, what would You call it?

Describe the voice that puts you down/puts you off.
What colour does it seem you? How does this creature move? Draw its portrait if you wish (but remember to add a false nose and silly glasses, perhaps an enormous bow tie and ridiculous hat when you've finished. Not quite so scary now, is it?!).
Think up a name to fit the voice that makes you doubt yourself and tries to stop you moving forward in your Life.

I call it *(cue bit of echoey reverb)* The....... Voice...... of...... Fear.......
(strange cackling may follow at this point...)

See, we've all been hurt a few times before. Quite a few

67

hundred times really. Been made to feel stupidsmallridiculous-nastyscaredbig-headedguilty and so like anyone, we're out to protect ourselves.

And, yep, this is the part of us that does not want us to get hurt again, no chance, no way.

So believing it's protecting you, it'll do anything to stop you from taking a risk, including using the same methods that worked so well to create the poor old scaredy cat with the funny voice in the first place.

And it didn't even exist till one day when you were about 6 months old and you were propped up on flowery cushions playing with your orange teddy when the big girl from next door came over into your garden and snatched it out of your chubby little hands and poked you in the tummy, quite hard.

Whaaaaaaaa!

What was that horrible feeling?

Come to think of it, it was a bit like when you were crying one night a few weeks later (how were you to know it was 3.30 in the morning?) and fancied a bit of a cuddle before you went back to sleep and your mum came in (looking pretty tired, now you think of it) and gave you a kiss on the nose, but no cuddle, and then, and this is the worst bit, said 'Night night' and LEFT THE ROOM AND SHUT THE DOOR!!! Whaaaaaaaaaaaaa! That felt really bad.

Okay, it might not have gone *exactly* like this, but you get the idea that when we arrive here, all ready to play, there's a point when suddenly we feel it, the tummy all clenched up, that sudden 'ooh, I feel really lonely and small...' feeling which has Fear at the centre of it, and pretty soon it develops a voice to protect you from exposing yourself to any other potential dangers out there.

See, what seems to be stopping you from doing loads of good stuff now, was really born out of a desire to look after you, and if it started off as your friend, with your best interests at heart, then there's real hope that with a bit of nurturing, some explaining, a few hugs and a perhaps a hot bubbly bath, we can go a long way to reassuring and transforming your Fear into the confident, strong and sensible friend you need now.

And there's a difference between a real fear – the feeling that alerts you to real danger, the hairs rising on the back of your neck feeling which is rare and should always be listened to – and a conditioned response to a certain situation, a fear you have learned over time. This is the clenched tummy reaction, and is one that may no longer be serving you well, one it might be time to explore and perhaps let go.

Take some time to list your fears. This might be a difficult thing to do so choose a time when you're feeling brave and have a bit of space.

I'm afraid of the dark/dogs/I'm afraid to lose/be alone/show others that I care.

Just list them as they come to you. Some you may know well, others may surprise you.

For now, it's enough to have looked your fears in the face. Say, out loud, 'I have been hurt and sometimes feel afraid. I'm still here. I am a brave and amazing person.' And say it again until you can say it without laughing. Say it until you mean it. Know that everyone is, in this way, the same.

If you want to share this with a supportive friend, look them in the eye and say, 'You have been hurt and sometimes feel afraid. You're still here. You are a brave and amazing person.'

And mean it.

Now give them, or yourself, a hug.

Chapter 11

Strength and Courage

'You gain strength, courage and confidence by every experience in which you really stop to look fear in the face. You are able to say to yourself, 'I have lived through this horror. I can take the next thing that comes along.'
Do the thing you think you cannot do.'
Eleanor Roosevelt

Okay now, this is no time to wallow in self-pity that gets us nowhere, but to recognise how strong we are by facing our fears. Our fears can be pretty useful because they highlight areas of our lives that need attention – loving, brave attention – and they give us the clues we need so that we might build ourselves up to the point where we feel strong enough to move through the fear.

The only real problem with fear is if we let it get the upper hand and control our every movement, because then we don't move anywhere and get stuck in our lives, and have you ever seen a two year old trying to pull their tractor (the wheels of which are tangled up in a skipping rope) out of the toy basket? Think frustration, think anger, think rage as they yank and scream and cry in their efforts to move what seems to be completely stuck.

Until they calm down and summon help or their big brother shows them how to untangle the mess, the tantrum will continue (unless they get distracted by the cat, who has wandered past to give the small human beasty a disdainful glance, and toddle off in pursuit, in which case the same thing will probably happen again next time they want to play tractors...)

It's those same emotions – the frustration, the anger, the rage – that build up within us if we ignore the opportunity for change that our fears give us and stay stuck when it would be much wiser to take a breath and try something new.

Next time you find yourself hesitating on the brink of trying something new, remember that you didn't learn to walk by refusing to get up again because you fell over the first time, too afraid to leave the safety of the sofa's edge ever again, worried about what other people might think of you. Nope. You got up again and again because when we're small there's no such thing as getting things wrong, only experimenting.

And remember that for every major discovery, every major achievement ever made there are mountains of scrunched up pieces of notepaper in wastebaskets, mountains of chalk dust created as another mathematical formula is rubbed out in frustration, rubber mountains the height of Everest as another athlete tries to break the record and wears through another pair of trainers in the process.

Think where we'd be if Nelson Mandela or JK Rowling had given in to their doubts and fears.

And before that pesky Voice of Fear jumps in to remind you that these people are far more amazing than you, just remember that they are people who just happen to be playing their Life with confidence and determination and belief in themselves despite the worst that their own Voice of Fear can think up to stop them in their tracks.

We each have our own Game to play that involves situations best suited to our own development as Players, and whether that means you end up being the representative of a nation, or the most sought-after mechanic this side of your hometown doesn't matter. There is no better or worst, only playing to the full despite the difficulties we face, or never even bothering to open the box in the first place.

The game you came here to play is a challenging one, and you designed it that way, surprisingly passing over others described on the box as *'Brilliantly boring! You'll not stop yawning with this one. So predictable, you might as well not bother!'*

Your game was designed to encourage you to grow and to learn, and so rather than getting paralysed by fear on Miss A Go, the idea was for you to take a breath, roll again, and move on.

(Caution: 'Yeah right!' moment coming up...)

Sometimes, the things that happen that feel so awful at the time can be times of huge development for us. *(Told you...)*

Well, remember the poking the cat in the eye incident? What useful lesson did you happen to learn about 2 seconds after that took place?
Exactly! Poke a cat in the eye, you get a nasty scratch.
Have you done it since? You haven't? Well, there you are.

Things that feel bad happen sometimes. They just do. But you can choose to be upset about this and give away your power, or you can choose to learn from that situation and see what it has to teach you. You can play the victim or you can be a warrior who has battle scars and is stronger and more powerful for having faced the fear.

It's simply a question of attitude.

Remember something that felt pretty bad. It might still hurt to recall it. Most importantly, what did you learn from that situation?

Can you see an opportunity for growth in there somewhere? Search really hard if it's not obvious at first.

My best friend Julie went off with that new girl and I was really devastated. It hurt a lot and made me feel scared of making new friends in case it happened again. After a while I made friends with Sacha and we have such a laugh. Looking back, I can see that I was a bit clingy with Julie and maybe that felt weird for her. I guess I learned how to trust someone else, which is a pretty big thing. It also showed me that I'm quite brave. I did make new friends even though I was a bit scared inside. I took a risk, and it paid off, which feels good. I guess I'm stronger now because of that, although it felt terrible at the time.

My dad's always wanted me to be this hard man, like I remember we'd not really hug or anything, but play fight and he'd teach me wrestling. Sometimes it really hurt. I've always been really small but I kind of knew I shouldn't say anything, so he'd be proud of me. When I started playing the guitar he laughed and did stupid impressions of me - it felt so bad, like I'd been punched. I felt like I couldn't talk to him about me or what I was doing. It was hard for a while, but I found out from my gran that my dad had been really bullied when he was my age. Suppose I understand where he's coming from a bit better. He still won't talk to me about music and he hasn't come to any of my gigs yet, but you never know...

And now congratulate yourself for having had the courage to touch a sore spot.

If we are full of fear it will affect every aspect of our lives, how we feel/behave/look/seem to others. Being this way affects our every moment and will ensure that, because we feel the world is a scary place, hey presto! the world, to a person full of a fear *is* a scary place.

Fear cuts down the choices you could take, and in every sense reduces you, limits you, squashes you into the little box it's made to keep things safe.

Bring to mind a person, living now or from a time in the past, whom you admire.

Make a list of words that describe them, think of the qualities they possess that you feel are worthy of your admiration.

Next time you find yourself in a difficult situation, ask yourself, 'What would so-and-so do in this situation?'

Imagine them giving you advice, or actually feel what it must be like to be them for a moment. See if this helps you to find a solution or a way through.

Remember that you can only see in others what is actually within yourself, maybe not shining out quite so brightly at the moment, but the potential is there, so build on it!

Chapter 12

All Change!

'Change is the constant, the signal for rebirth, the egg of the phoenix.'
Christina Baldwin

Sometimes our fears seem scarier than they really are. They become FEARS, get sharp teeth and we try to stay out of their way. We put them into boxes, big strong boxes with enormous padlocks and try to forget where we hid the keys. No use though, because just when we think we've got rid of them for good, they start rumbling and disturbing us in the middle of the night until one day, that's it! You rummage around to find the keys, fumble with the lock with shaking fingers, throw open the lid of the box and wait for the worst. You can't see anything. Okay, you've still got your eyes closed, but slowly, you open them and peer inside. What you see now is looking back at you, pretty pleased that you finally decided to meet up at last after all this time, and reminds you why it was put into the box in the first place. You remember how you'd been much younger then and what happened had made you feel just awful. But that was a long time ago, and you're stronger now, and you can look your Fear in the face till it shrinks and doesn't look quite as scary any more.

Suddenly you realise that the story you'd been telling about yourself, the 'I'm scared of spiders/water/everyone' story just isn't true any more. It had been your story once, but you can see now how it had kind of got stuck and just wasn't true any more, hadn't been true for ages, years even, but you'd been living your life as if it were. Weird.

So, time to rewrite that old story and let go of the old fears. Things we do/think/believe over and over again become habits and remember how difficult it was to stop biting your nails/sucking your thumb/avoiding the cracks in the pavement? Difficult, maybe, but definitely possible.

Fear is about hiding behind closed doors; this is about opening them up and seeing what's really out there for you.

So, you feel like you're serving a life sentence, bound to your fears? Then go for early release, making your life sentences ones that empower you and make your life more of the fun, exciting adventure it was always meant to be!

Transform your fear into an opportunity to grow and form a short sentence to hold this new idea. For example, you feel scared of spiders, or have done in the past. Your new sentence might go something like, *'Spiders are tiny compared to me, quite harmless, and my fear is in the past. I am letting it go.'* Repeat it until you believe it.

Maybe you're afraid of speaking in front of others, and so your new sentence might be, *'What's the worse that can happen? Nothing will keep me from speaking my truth. My voice is proud of what it has to say. I can speak out.'*

In any challenging situation (spidery or otherwise), keep breathing and aim to move through the whole experience without giving the fear that may still linger there for a while too much attention.

Focus instead on your new sentence, on keeping your breathing slow and steady.

Keep going, and when the moment has passed, don't forget to tell yourself, 'Hey! Well done! I did pretty well there!'

We learn to be afraid and know how to do that really well, and so it can seem a bit tricky to suddenly change how things are overnight, but it is possible to help yourself learn a new, more positive habit. Each time the fear tries to get in the way of who you really are, stop, take a breath and say (either out loud, if you feel the bus queue can take it, or silently to yourself), 'That was then. I am stronger now. This is NOW!'

Moving your body – stamping your feet or shaking out your hands – helps too as it moves you physically from a stuck place that you might be in. Sometimes all it takes is to remind yourself that it is NOW! that you're dealing with, and the short blast of the word NOW! can wake you up to the present moment, which is where we all really want to be.

Fear is the part of you that is stuck in the past, wasting all your strength clinging onto the rocks whilst the river rushes past you. Our lives are about change, we know that, and if we resist that change it can feel pretty terrible. Change means movement, it means growth, and it will happen, however hard we try to resist. In fact, the harder we resist, the harder and more uncomfortable it feels as change tries to force its way through.

Sometimes, jumping off the rock you're clinging to can seem like madness, but if you do it and go with the flow of the rushing river, it might just be that it's about the most fun/ exhilarating/ liberating thing you've ever experienced, and look! just that bit further along you see a raft that you clamber onto and you actually start enjoying the sights and sounds from your new vantage point, floating along until, see that spot a bit further along the river bank? That's where you're going to land and start exploring.

Life is a bit like this. We do something, we test the water, there's a reaction and we then decide if we ever want to try that again. Our body, our emotions, our very spirit, (the bit that shines us up, that makes us who we truly are, that you feel in your heart when you are doing something that is absolutely RIGHT and you know it), work together to help us learn these lessons by letting us know if something feels bad/healthy/wonderful/scary, supporting us as we decide what choice to make next time. If we don't get the lesson first time around, you can guarantee that there will be another opportunity to test yourself coming up soon.

Life is a Game, and you have to learn enough to pass through to the next level, and until you can negotiate the bridge with the slimy troll under it, you're forever destined to get as far as that bridge and no further. But you get scared, just getting near it? That's okay, feel scared and then ask yourself if this is an old, conditioned fear getting in your way. If you suspect it is, move on and through the fear to a new place.

Idea: Tried talking to the troll? Maybe he's a bit fed up with everyone thinking he's a monster just because he looks how you think a monster would look. Give him a break. Maybe all that gurgling shouty raging he does is Trollspeak for, 'That'll be £2.50 to cross the magic bridge, O respected traveller'?

Ah, you tried that too, and have the scars to prove it. Mmm.

Maybe you were too focused on the troll to notice the hot air balloon that is hiding, as only a hot air balloon can, behind the small hawthorn tree just to the left of the scary bridge? Just a thought. There's more than one way to cross a river, after all...

So remember, next time that little voice starts offering its unwanted advice and you start talking yourself out of some new opportunity, try this...say firmly, 'Thanks for your input, and I know you're only trying to help but I'd like you to be quiet now'. It'll be so surprised that it probably will.

Then take a deep breath and go ahead and discover how it feels to take a chance.

It works out, you feel fantastic. Things don't go so well, take another breath and reassure yourself that you've been brave and strong and that this alone is enough to get you through any disappointment you might feel.

And when the euphoria or the disappointment has faded, as it always will if you let it pass through you and don't cling onto it, it'll be time for the next challenge, and then the next, and the next...

Chapter 13

Positive Reactions

'When you are content to simply be yourself and don't compare or compete, everybody respects you.' Lao-Tzu

You've got toothache/sprained your ankle/got something scratchy in your eye.

You wake up, it's the first thing you feel. At breakfast, it's impossible to enjoy your porridge because your tooth/ankle/eye hurts. It's all you can think about, all you feel, all day.

And by the end of the day you're so consumed by it that you snap at the little boy who lives next door and who accidentally kicked his ball into your garden. Who does he think he is, asking for you to retrieve it for him? Doesn't he know that you're in pain?

If you feel pain, it's so much harder to be pleasant to others. It can make life seem so difficult and it's pretty hard to enjoy things when you don't feel like yourself and everything is so pain-full. By making it our mission to sort out the yukky stuff as we feel it inside before it ends up hurting anyone else, we're really doing our bit to clean up the planet – we wouldn't chuck our rubbish all over the place and expect someone else to clear it up, but that's exactly what we do if we go out into the world in a bad mood and have a go at some innocent bystander who happens to wander our way; not only are we not feeling any better, but we're just passing the energy on and it'll get passed on and on until it reaches someone who knows how to transform it into something more positive and healthy.

The calmer and more centred you are, the more likely you are to make a positive choice and avoid reacting and getting caught up in the emotion that colours a situation. This doesn't mean you don't care. Rescuing your best friend from a hole in the ground? You might choose (a) to jump in, get dragged down and both end up shouting for help, or (b) to take a deep breath, step back and respond from a calmer, more detached place. And then get a rope. Avoid getting pulled in yourself. If you're stuck in a heap at the bottom of a pit, your options, in terms of how much genuine help you can expect to offer, are severely limited.

So there's a link between what we do, or what we don't do, and what happens next.

Just ask your friendly neighbourhood science teacher, and as well as being extremely pleased that you're taking an interest in a subject close to their heart (we hope, otherwise they're in the wrong job and you may need to lend them a copy of this book…), they will tell you that every action has a reaction.

Everything we do, everything we say, everything we think leads us somewhere else, and because we all choose, moment to moment, what to do, say or think, we are ultimately in charge of how we feel.

But, hark, I hear some spluttering…okay, okay, yes, I know you didn't make your science teacher slam the staffroom door in your face when all you were about to do was ask an innocent question. This is true. You were then faced, in a split second with an array of options. How about kicking the door and shouting an expletive? Might have more extreme consequences than muttering something rude under your breath, but you still feel cross and angry and bitter in both cases.

This time, your game-playing practice must be paying off because you took a deep breath and chose to think, 'Must have a lot on his plate. Looked a bit tired. Anyway, I'll ask Chris. Bet he'll know.'

Taking responsibility for ourselves, our thoughts and actions is vital if we're to be in our true power, play our own game, and let's face it, it's just less messy too.

Next time someone is rude to you, try taking a breath and avoid getting pulled into their bad mood.

Choose to respond in a calm, detached but caring way if you can.

As you leave the situation, remember what it's like to feel so yukky inside that you lash out at others and recognise that this person must be going through a hard time to behave in that way.

You might want to send them a little burst of positive energy to help them through it.

See how this works for you.

And it's worth remembering that the pain we all feel at times isn't always due to some physical cause.

Let's zoom back to a time when grey polyester V-necks, skipping rope at break time and ninja turtle sandwich boxes played a big part in our lives...(Why, in Heaven's name,' we gasp as one, 'would anyone choose to do this?'

Well, it's educational, believe me...)

Yes, we're back in Junior school and Mr Neering, the scourge of Year 6, with his booming voice and particular way of making you squirm if you get a question wrong is striking fear into the hearts of even the hardest ten year olds.

It's a beautiful morning outside and whilst you should be silently considering Rain Fall Levels and their impact on wine production in Alsace, surprisingly your attention is wandering. You look out of the window and your eye is caught by a small grey-haired lady in a flowery dress making her way across the playground.

Suddenly her cheery face appears at the window of your classroom door. She appears to be struggling with the latch. Mr Neering, obviously enthralled by Essential Geography For The Young Person, is unaware of this, and of the fact that things are about to take an interesting turn, for all concerned...

You raise your hand. 'Sir?'

He looks up. 'Yes? What is it? Constructing a simple graph proving difficult?'

'Um, no Sir. But there's someone at the door, Sir.'

And then the door flew open and the old lady bustled in.

'Neville, dear!' she cried, and kissed a rather flustered-looking Mr Neering on the forehead.

'Neville, dear!' (so you really did hear it right the first time, and you are strangely delighted) 'You forgot your packed lunch leaving all in a rush this morning, dashing off without even cleaning your teeth. Well, we can't have my boy going hungry, not with his rumbly old tum, now can we? Here it is, deary, and I've popped in a Walnut Whip too. Your favourite.'

And with that, a squeeze of his hand and a 'Bye bye, love!' she was gone.

Everything was quiet. All eyes were on Sir, Sir Neville Neering, for some long, long seconds.

He was blushing, and his hair was in his eyes where she had ruffled it. He smoothed his hair, coughed a short cough, and said in a voice the class had never heard before, 'Um, well, that's enough. Settle down, now. Yes.'

And you did, amazed and wondering if, just maybe, he could be a real person after all.

Poor Neville. Because, you see, what no one else knew was that he didn't even want to be a teacher in the first place, but it was in the family after all and 'it's a respectable way to earn a living, Neville.' Did Neville say this? He did not, but his dad did, loads of times, and remember that bit at the start of the book about wanting to please other people and fit in? It's a powerful feeling.

Neville had always loved painting, and some of his watercolours had even received some praise...'What? Those wishy washy old things? Come on, be serious. This is the real world, and you can hardly call being an artist a real job, can you?'

See, everyone's got their own Voice of Fear, some more muscley than others. Sometimes they use the words and phrases you've heard other people say, and sometimes they make up their own. And incidentally, look at the use of that rhetorical question, just aching for him to drop his head and resign his life away. Sly work, Oh Sneaky Voice of Fear.

As it happened, Neville was a teeny bit jealous of all the kids laughing and messing about and being ten. All that secretly wanting to have a bit of fun but forcing himself into a suit and being scary was bound to take its toll.

So, Neville ended up a bit of a bully. All bullies hope to gain some sort of energy from the bullying situation – it might be the fear or admiration of others, but whatever it is, it's energy that they hope will fill the gap inside them. Yep. There's an empty space inside every bully that's crying out for love and attention and they'll use anything that comes their way to fill it, even if it belongs to someone else.

Like a vampire after your lunch money, a bully siphons off

energy that doesn't belong to them, but the feeling of being big and strong doesn't last, because unless the feeling good comes from inside yourself, from inside the very heart of you, nothing will make things right.

True personal power is balanced and healthy – it is strong without needing to show it by flexing its muscles at someone else's expense. If you feel secure in your own power, you respect yourself and automatically respect others; it's almost impossible to misuse your power when you are awake and playing your game with confidence because making others feel bad would make you feel bad. That simple!

So, until Neville digs out his easel and gets busy with his watercolours, he's always going to feel scrunched up and just plain wrong inside because he's not doing what his heart, the part that makes him truly Neville, really needs.

Fear has so much to answer for, and it's at the root of most of all poor/careless/violent behaviour. In fact, any behaviour that isn't positive or creative or the healthiest choice in any situation is due to some measure of fear squirming its way in there and twisting things up.

It's true that nine times out of ten, the person who made you look stupid in front of your mates wasn't consciously aware that you would then lose the confidence to ask out your friend's gorgeous friend, and even the one who laughed at you when you said you wanted to be an artist didn't really want your hopes of going to Art school to shrivel to nothing, not unless they were feeling really mean and bitter inside, and believe me, that has nothing to do with you, but you guessed it, everything to do with their own Fears wobbling their way out into the conversation.

Sometimes we just wander innocently into the path of someone who has a whole load of sadness/anger/twisted yucky stuff to cope with and sometimes it spills out all over you, or me, or the next person in the post office queue.

This strange and rather messy phenomenon can be explained by realising that, as we know, everyone has their very own Voice of Fear that, when challenged, will prompt them to put others down and prevent change at all costs, because change, to someone full of Fear, is very scary indeed. Far safer to be in a place you know well, even if it is boring/frightening/unhealthy because at least it's comfy and predictable and will place no new demands on you.

If you are full of fear, making sure others don't change is the best bet, because then everyone stays where they should be and you can pretend that change isn't useful/inevitable/absolutely vital. And to make sure others don't change, you make them doubt themselves by feeding their own fears, undermining their confidence and preying on their vulnerabilities.

Eek. This sounds awful, and it's worth repeating that most people don't even realise they are doing this. It's going on subconsciously, perhaps underneath the smiley exterior and bright-sounding questions that leave you feeling just that bit odd but you're not sure why – what's happening is, whilst it all seems positive on the outside, the energy being sent your way isn't smiley and bright at all, but perhaps a little jealous and insecure.

It happens because we compare ourselves to others, believing that someone else being creative and amazing means we are smaller and useless in comparison. We want to feel good about ourselves, and because our lives at times can seem like competitions, with having to be the favourite/brightest/best-looking all the time, if we're not the best, then we feel rubbish, unloved and kind of worthless.

Well, here's the good bit. Our lives are not competitions, whatever anyone says. There may be competitions in them, but a round of Bingo every now and then isn't going to harm anyone.

We are not here to compete with others, to win, or to lose. We are here to play our own game, dance to the tunes we like and to enjoy sharing a few moves with others. It's that simple, and that difficult at the same time.

To stamp on a new shoot that is struggling through the soil and threatening to look more incredible than you is a step that only really makes us feel better for a moment, because whilst that shoot might be destroyed for a while, there are always others to keep an eye out for, and if you're unable to rest until every one is dealt with, you're in for a restless, pointless kind of life. Worth bearing in mind too, that that little shoot can be incredibly resilient, and if its growth is blocked in one area, it will re-route and pop up somewhere else.

Just take a walk along any pavement and marvel at the green shoots that manage to force their way up through the tiniest crack in the tarmac.

Warning: Doing this may change your life. You may never look at the humble dandelion in the same light again.

Next time a bully crosses your path, or the next time you feel tempted to sneer/mock/laugh a mean little laugh, even at yourself, stop for a moment and ask – where is this behaviour or this feeling coming from?

What sadness/anger/emptiness is behind all this?

Replace the words sneery/aggressive/mean with scared/jealous/unhappy and know that fear is at the root of it all.

Take a step back from the situation, take a breath, and see things with a wider lens. It might help.

Chapter 14

Digging Deep

'Our deepest fear is not that we are inadequate. Our deepest fear is that we are powerful beyond measure.'
Marianne Williamson

So we've all been there, being mean to our little brother, pretending that the supply teacher smelled bad (and Miss Walker, I am really, really sorry about that) and if we are aware that that behaviour is coming from a bit of a sad/angry/needy place within us, then we can do something about it. Yep! It's time to get to know our meanies and give them some love!

But wait a minute, all this hugging and stuff. All this positive-thinking business. It's just not cool, is it? Well, it's just not cool to what? Feel good about who you are? Enjoy yourself? Not cool to care about yourself and others and what you do, to want to have as good a time as possible, to really go for all the things that you've always wanted?

It is difficult to go against what others are doing, and in our society at the moment there seem to be only a few accepted ways to behave/look/be.

Once we realise that those are just the ideas dreamt up by people caught up in a huge industry that cares more about money than it does about our hearts and souls, and if we acknowledge that this dream wraps itself around us all using any medium it can to reach us, then we then have the power to stop dreaming someone else's dream and wake up to our own lives, to our very selves and really feel alive.

And you've only got to try this to know it's true. Don't take my word for it. Never take anyone's word for it, but if you try it and it works, then what have you got to lose? A dream that was getting boring anyway? A dream that didn't really have you at its heart?

Alarm bells going off all over the place? Bleary-eyed persons scratching their heads as if emerging from a long, long sleep? Good! Then wakey wakey, rise and really shine!

Waking up to ourselves and becoming more aware of what's going on is like taking a step back to view a scene more clearly; by doing this we can see the relationships between things, how things are put together and how they work. Becoming more informed about how the game of life works is pretty useful to those of us who are taking part in it this time around.

'Why am I doing this?' is a question that it's good to ask ourselves at least once in a while.

Why, for example, do I keep getting up to wander around the kitchen, finding myself rooting in the sultana jar or buttering crackers? Is it, perhaps, that I am responding to my body's desperate nutritional need for dried fruits and crispbread? I think not. Could it possibly be that I am putting off the inevitable, the actual sitting down at the kitchen table and getting some of these words down on the page? Could it be that I am, actually, procrastinating and the wandering around pretending that I'm hungry is nothing more than an avoidance technique?

Mmmm.

Digging deeper, all I've got to do is ask, so why am I doing this? Why am I avoiding the writing bit? I've got all the ideas, I love this book and want to see it bounce around alive and happy in other people's hands, so..?

Well, and this is the squirmy, not-so-comfortable but the real and interesting part, it's because maybe I'm a bit scared. Scared that it won't be good enough, scared that I'm not good enough.

Oooh, that's interesting. Keep digging... Good enough for what?

Well, if my words aren't right, and I'm not good enough then people won't like me and no one will love me.

And?

And it'll be horrible.

Why?

Because, because I want to be loved. I don't like it if people don't like me. It scares me.

Could you, by any chance, be the one who got poked in the stomach and had their orange teddy snatched? And who was left to cry (we appreciate that back then 6 minutes felt like a lifetime) that night when your poor mum was exhausted?

Er, maybe.

And this led to you being afraid to be on your own, even when being on your own was way better for you than being with some of the people you ended up with along the way?

Might have done.

Aha! Mystery of the avoidance technique unraveled.

See, so much of our lives are like little mysteries for us to solve and if we approach our problems, our strange habits and the things that just don't feel right as a detective might, we can see beyond the surface to the reasons that lie buried deep, deep down. We can begin to understand that we may have been affected by someone else and that they, in turn, acted in a certain way because of things that had happened to them. When you start to become aware of this, your mind starts to spiral a bit and you realise that we're all connected to others and everything everyone does/says/even thinks has an effect on everything else out there. Like one big cosmic game of domino rally. Phew.

It can be an interesting and sometimes emotional journey, facing up to those fears and digging down to where they all began, like a puzzle or a maze we wander till we find the scary monster at the centre. And when we confront the beast, rather than just roaring and biting off our heads, they usually have some lesson or story or a magic object that will be useful to us, and we return home stronger and richer from having dared to visit.

> Throw a pebble into a lake.
> Throw it and watch the ripples that can go for miles, all from the single stone, and continue long after that pebble has disappeared beneath the surface.

What do I do now, now that I've discovered that my fear of not being loved is stopping me from being as creative as I can? Well, I'm not going to stand here and feel sorry for myself any more, because that's only going to bring more situations and people to me that keep me stuck in the old pattern and make me feel sorry for myself all over again. Once we learn something, it's time to move on to the next class, unless you want to take the same lesson over and over and over...

The only way out of all this is to stop looking outside myself for love and encouragement, because now I know that everyone is trying to sort out their own stuff and is bound to disappoint me if I expect something from them that they just aren't ready/able/in the right place to give. It's great, if there's someone to share what I'm going through, but if not, then that's fine too.

We all come to this point if we're lucky (even if it might be a particularly uncomfortable and difficult time that brings us here); we arrive at the place where we realise that actually it's up to us to choose how to respond to situations rather than reacting negatively to other people's behaviour/lack of interest/weird looks across the dinner table. It's about taking back the power we have been placing in other people's hands; rather than it being 'all their fault', we can choose to take that responsibility back for ourselves, and a mighty liberating thing to do it is too.

If we feel that we 'need' something from others, it's the signal to look to that place inside ourselves that feels empty and is in real need of some attention.

It's important to realise that you have to be able to give yourself the love, the nurturing, the encouragement that you might once have felt only others could give you, because you will only receive from others what you believe you are worth, and the more you value yourself, the better you feel and actually, though you feel less 'needy', the more you will receive from people around you. Weird, but true.

Tuning forks is the answer. Yep, if a tuning fork is struck and sounds a note, all other tuning forks in the area (amazing how many there might be, lurking in dark corners, you know...) will start to vibrate to the same note. And if you're wandering around full of negative thoughts and feelings, the great cosmic orchestra will start to play in tune with you and your life will be full of all sorts of negative, unhappy tunes that get on your nerves and set your teeth on edge like fingernails down a blackboard.

So, raise your vibration, make the song you're singing a happier, healthier one and things around you will start to change: opportunities come your way, suddenly people seem much friendlier, situations you had felt stuck in start to free up and change for the better. Sounds good! It's true – and if you've never set eyes, let alone ears, on a tuning fork, go to your music teacher and ask them to show you how this works.

And then someone asks, 'But what's the point? There's bad stuff happening all over the place – children dying, earthquakes, war. Shouldn't we spend our time thinking about those things a bit more? Isn't it selfish to be happy all the time?'

The only answer can be that by focusing too long on the bad stuff that happens in this world, our energy becomes depressed and negative so we actually create more negative energy in the world.

The only way we can affect anyone, anywhere, in a positive way is to make our thoughts and actions as positive as we can and this has the very real effect of bringing more positivity into the world as a whole, the world that we are all part of because we are all connected.

If you truly want to help those who are in trouble, avoid indulging in the media fest that whips up negative emotional energy around what they see as a 'sensational story' to attract viewers and readers – this only creates feelings of fear and helplessness in us all.

Choose instead to focus on a more positive outcome for all those involved and send them love in your thoughts or prayers. Join an action group working for positive change in that area.

Know that you *can* do something, and make it something positive.

Chapter 15

Light up your Life

'Keep away from the people who try to belittle your ambitions. Small people always do that, but the really great make you feel that you, too, can be great.'
Mark Twain

So if fear is what we get when we're cut off from what we really are, cut off from that shiny spirit of ours, then how in the name of all that sparkles are we to get back what we've lost and light up our lives a bit?

We all feel tired and cranky when we're not getting the nourishment we need and the things you love to do are like food for your soul. You need to do them. It is necessary, absolutely vital to do creative stuff that links you in to that spirity place.

Go even a few days without doing the things you love and how do you feel? Exactly!

So just what is it that you love to do?
What makes you feel more like You?
List all the things you do or see that make you feel good.

I love walking in the woods...colours can make my mouth water...I like taking things apart to see how they work...listening to my grandma's stories feels like home...making bread feels good...
I feel truly alive dancing when I know no one's watching...

Aim to do at least one of these things this week, if not right now!
Experiment by noting how you feel before and after your session; if you feel better, more energised and positive then you've proved to yourself that doing whatever it is, is good for you!

And if you could do anything in the world, what would it be?

Ballet, bricklaying, bonsai? And don't let anyone tell you that you can't try all three, if that's what you want to do. The idea that 'Well, you can't be good at everything, now, can you?' comes from a place that believes that it's only worth doing something if you can be *seen* to be good at it, or be 'the best'.

But what about being creative for its own sake? Enjoying ourselves as we express who we are is what Life is about; it's vital, in the truest sense of the word!

Don't worry what anyone else might think about what you want to do, this is your own heart's desire and following it will lead you right back where you belong.

It's the map, the compass, the carrot on the stick that will lead you where you are meant to be, comfy and cosy, inside your own skin. It will lead you back to yourself.

> Over the next few weeks build up a collection of pictures, images, textures, leaves, words and phrases that speak to you, that call, Hey you! and won't shut up until you cut them out of the magazine or pick them up.
>
> You might choose pictures of places you want to visit one day; rivers you'd like to swim in; someone skydiving, wild against a vast blue sky; favourite animals; buildings you'd like to explore...
>
> Add a line from your favourite song; a wrapper from the sweets your granddad crunched ferociously when he gave up smoking aged 81, two years before he died; a shell from the beach that smells of adventure...

Collect anything that says something positive and beautiful and creative about your life, as it is now, and how, in your heart of hearts, you want it to be in the future.

This is really important, because what we focus on tends to come to us, be it good stuff, bad stuff, or just plain weird stuff.

As you know, everything that exists first started out as a tiny thought in someone's head.

Take this to its logical extreme and you realise that everything, every single thing and every single situation exists because someone created it.

Someone once coined a rather natty phrase to describe this phenomenon, saying, 'Where thought goes, energy flows'. And it's true, it does.

Surround yourself with unhappy, bitter, unhealthy stuff and

there's no prize for guessing how you're going to feel after a while, which is why it's really important to focus on as many positive, healthy things as possible. And no way is this living some sort of airy-fairy smiley fantasy.

It takes real guts and determination to live a positive, healthy Life and enjoy the game you came here to play.

So, when you feel it's the right time, and you've collected enough, set aside an evening or two to create a collage of your images, leaving a space in the centre for the most important image of all, one of you looking smiley and happy. Stick it onto gold paper, make it special.
Place your collage somewhere you can look at it often and feel your spirits lift.

This is your life.
Your past, your future and your present, as in something you're living right now, and something that has been given to you, an incredible gift.
Say thank you, and enjoy. You deserve it.

And if you're lucky, it might be that there are people around you to encourage and support you, to reflect back to you this image of yourself as the dancer/artist/carpenter/explorer you want to be, who lives inside you and is awaiting expression. However, sometimes we can feel that this kind of support is not available to us. In this case, it's important to nurture your dream and be careful with it. See it as a tiny seedling that needs care and attention to grow, and keep it safe from heavy boots and unthinking hands.

Only share your dream with those you know will be able to feel good for you, and encourage you. Remember too that if it's a true dream and you follow what's in your heart, it's guaranteed that sooner or later you will meet others who will support and inspire you, that you will find yourself in situations that feed your dream and its development. The most important thing is that you believe in yourself, in your right to dream and be who you know in your heart you can be. It is this powerful feeling that kind of shifts your world and trains its focus on achieving your goal.

This week, do one thing that supports your dream.

It might be starting to save for tickets to go to the ballet, going to the library to check out the autobiography of that amazing explorer, walking in the woods and spending some time drawing what you see there or asking if you can borrow a camera from school to see if photography is your thing.

It doesn't have to be a huge deal, but by doing something, anything, that feeds the positive excited feeling you get when you think about doing what you want to do, you're sending a clear message to yourself, to others and the wider world that you believe in something, and as we know, whatever we believe, whether it's 'I'm not worth anything' or 'I can lead an exciting, creative life full of possibilities' will do its best to come true for us.

Intention is like an arrow and a strong, clear intention will do anything to reach its target. By making sure our intentions are clear, our lives become less messy and more focused.

Tomorrow, when you wake up, set an intention for the day. *I mean to walk instead of getting the bus/I intend to be more relaxed around my brother /I'm going to spend some time by myself, just being quiet for once.*

Some people like to make this a bit special by setting aside a moment to focus on their goal, maybe lighting a candle or spending a minute silently imagining themselves doing whatever it is they're intending to do. Again, this helps to strengthen your intention because you're seeing it as important and giving it more energy in the form of time and attention.

However things go, just note how you feel, and set your next intentions accordingly!

Chapter 16

The Choice is Yours

'To be nobody-but-yourself - in a world which is doing its best, day and night, to make you everybody else - means to fight the hardest battle which any human being can ever fight; and never stop fighting.'
e. e. cummings

Today you're stressed. So stressed that your head is actually hurting and you've just shouted at your little brother/cat/fridge (because you flung it open in a desperate search for sugar-laden carbohydrate snacks to make you feel better and the tomato sauce flew out and smashed all over the kitchen floor...) Assorted family members and pets are now cowering upstairs to avoid the wailing/swearing/screams of rage that accompany your cleaning-up effort.

You slump onto the sofa, in the hope that daytime TV will provide you with the answers you seek. You watch Sarah who, in front of an invited and excited audience, attacks her (ex) best friend because she knew that she knew that Dave, her (whose?) boyfriend (ex, obviously), knew this new girl at work. *And when we say 'knew', we mean really knew, eh viewers?!*

'Join us after the break - and let's hope it's not too serious; you've got quite a punch there, Sarah! – as we delve deeply into the world of pasta shell jewellery-making and ask,
'Eye-catching necklace or tea time staple?'
We can't wait!'

You feel strangely let down by today's chat show. Let down, depressed, confused. You seem unable to reach for the remote control and are innocently bombarded with adverts for the very same sugar-laden carbohydrate snack that started all this in the first place. Didn't it?

Before you can work out why you feel so angry and upset you begin to wonder if it really is time to start thinking about joining a slimming club/using wrinkle cream/investing in male grooming products as you suddenly start to feel rather insecure, comparing yourself to the grinning, gorgeous nearly-naked TV people who live in the sun and have loads of friends and speedboats.

Perhaps you really do need that chemical-laden, unnaturally perfumed gunk. You could smear it on to be absorbed by your skin, confusing your body as it tries to work out what to do with all those bizarre substances. Mmmm. But at least you'd Be Happy!!!

Perhaps the passport to your dreams really does lie inside shiny red packaging? Maybe it'd be different this time so that when you bought it and got it home, the excitement would last and the promises they made you really would come true.

Actually, it's worth remembering at this point that the company who want you to buy it will probably not have your best interests at heart.

What?!

Okay. Maybe this is too cynical. Maybe they really do want you to be happy, to fulfill your dreams, to be confident and responsible and independent. Yes. Absolutely. Quite right.

Well, er, maybe not too confident, because then you might be happy with who you are and not need the armour that their badge/logo/club provides.

And maybe not too responsible for yourself, because then you might realise that your happiness depends entirely on what you can provide for yourself, things that are usually free, and not on the things they can sell you.

And while we're at it, maybe not too independent either as that might mean you don't need them at all to be happy, and we wouldn't want you believing that now, would we?

It's something we might all remember as we watch TV / read a magazine / catch sight of a billboard / are glued to our seat in the cinema for twenty minutes before the film and are force-fed adverts that have cost thousands, if not millions of pounds, to develop and reach you. And why might a company spend so much money to persuade you to buy its products?

They know that the visual image is incredibly powerful. Combine this with a voice-over spoken by someone who seems to really care about us, perhaps some music to manipulate our emotions further and a vulnerable state brought about by some skillful preying on our fears and insecurities, and what you have is a potion that will work its magic on a large percentage of what the company calls its target audience.

They pay up, and everyone's happy.

Aren't they?

Hum.

Choose to study three adverts today as if you are a detective. Ask yourself who the advert is aimed at. *Young men / older women / single or married / children...*

Be as specific as you can, even giving your person a name, an address, describing how they dress/eat/feel today...

Work out how the advert is trying to persuade the target to buy the product. How might the music/ colours/ scenery/ images used affect the target audience? Which words or phrases are repeated, and why?

What's the message of the advert that the company wants its target audience to swallow?

Do you, as the detective, believe there are hidden messages that work between the lines to manipulate the target and make them feel a certain way?

Remember that, as in every area of your life, you have the power to choose, and as a consumer you have the power to choose which companies to support. There are companies out there who really care about the people who work for them and the planet that provides them with resources and can still turn an ethically-grown profit. Make it your mission to become aware of how the companies you buy from treat people and our planet and what they do with their profits.

Money is just energy in a physical form – choose to be aware what you are giving your precious energy to.

And if you want to avoid the line of fire?

Choose to switch off/look away/close your eyes and stick your fingers in your ears when adverts come on.

Choose not to read magazines that promote the idea that there is only one way to look/eat/smell.

Choose to be aware when someone is trying to manipulate you, making you feel a certain way so they can get something from you.

Choose to say, 'No thanks!' and walk away.

Clearly, a lot of this is about appearance, how things look on the surface, and at the moment our culture seems particularly obsessed with this, which has led to a lot of unhappy people wandering around from shop to shop looking for designer sunglasses to make them feel better. It's not going to happen, not until they begin to realise that how they feel depends on somewhere much deeper inside them, and if they follow the guidance from that place, they'll feel better on the outside.

There's a difference between respecting yourself and your body, and only wearing certain clothes because the magazines tell you that's what's acceptable. Find out what suits you, what you feel good in because it's an expression of you and your uniqueness. Wear purple if you want to! Wear your comfy trainers even if they don't have a little mark on them that tells everyone they cost eighty quid! Wear the turtle earrings your gran gave you because you love your gran more than you care about the ridiculous whims of fashion...

Choose to wear something you like today, feeling confident that you have made your own choice without being influenced by an industry that focuses too much of its undoubted creative talent in unhealthy directions.

Someone sneers at your choice? Let their fear of being different, because that's what it really is, bounce off the armour that being true to yourself provides. Know that genuinely respecting yourself will eventually lead to the genuine respect of others who will somehow recognise a strength and authenticity about you that will hopefully inspire them too.

Start being you from the inside out, and not the outside in.

And if you're still stuck on the sofa in a daze? You're doomed to consume another...

A picture of someone with a glazed expression, slumped on a sofa in front of the TV appears on the screen. Probably another advert for sleeping aids/high interest loans/expensive holidays...

But hold on a minute, haven't you seen that face somewhere before..?

(Concerned, kindly-sounding voice over) 'Feeling angry? Upset? Your head full of thoughts spinning round and round with nowhere to go? Taking it out on everything around you and need to relax before you scare the cat away for good?

Then it's time for some action.

Those deep breaths you've read about? Take three of them, right now.

Calmer?

(Person on sofa nods)

That's great.

Want to take control of the situation and emerge as a lighter, happier you?

(They nod again, interested...)

Then get up and move that body!

Yes! Years of research has shown that moving your body and getting some fresh air helps to reduce the signs of stress that we all experience at certain times. In fact, in a highly scientific study of people buying cat food in their local greengrocer, 97% agreed that their cats preferred them to take a brisk walk round the block rather than arrive home stressed and angry.

(Person on sofa looks a trifle guilty as a mournful miaow issues off camera)

Whether it's a walk in the park, a jog to the corner and back or simply going out into the back yard for some deep breathing, it all helps to slow down your racing mind so that your next steps can be positive ones.

Take our advice. It's absolutely free so you don't pay us anything now, in fact there's no need to pay us anything, ever!

(Person now standing in garden looks amazed)

It's true!

Take you for a ride? Never! Take yourself for a walk, and you'll feel better.

Guaranteed!'

Advert ends. Chat show begins. You stand up and switch it off.

From this moment, you know that you can choose what to let into your head, your heart, your life.

You walk around the block, breathing calmly. Your fists unclench, your pace slows. You notice a blackbird singing on a branch and you watch it for a while until it flies off. You think of the reasons why you were so stressed in the first place and realise it can all be sorted out. You smile a bit. Home again, you let yourself in and apologise to your mum and to the cat.

All is well. Well, better.

Chapter 17

Free!

*'I want to sing like birds sing, not worrying about who hears or
what they think.'*
Rumi

*The channel we were tuning into previously seems to have been
experiencing some interference. We are sorry for any confusion this may
have caused and are glad to say that normal service resumes at this
point. More mind-numbing daytime TV interspersed with colourful and
exciting attempts to persuade you to hand over your cash follows shortly.*

Phew. Thank goodness for that. All that sensible, free advice that
actually works and supports us as we play our difficultsometime-
shazardousamazing games in life was making me feel strange. But
strange in a good way. And there are many other good ideas the
advertisers won't be telling you because then you might not need
what they are so desperate to sell you.

If you're feeling stuck, or confused inside a situation and can't see
a way out, what has happened is that your energy – the stuff that
everything is made up of, including us, our feelings, thoughts and
emotions – has literally got stuck, or confused, and the best way
to move the energy is to do something physical to shift it. It won't
sort out the root of the problem, but it will certainly help you see
things more clearly and help you approach the situation with a
fresher, more detached perspective.

So, try singing! As loudly as you can, in the shower, in your room.

Anywhere.

Go for a bike ride and let the air rush over you, washing your tangled-up bits all clear again.

Sit by the river, pick up a pebble, whisper your worries into it and throw it in as far as you can knowing it will be rinsed clean.

Go out in the rain and let the water wash your anxieties away.

Listen to some ridiculous comedy on CD, or watch a funny film. Laughing will shift your energy and make your heart lighter probably faster than anything.

Grab a spade and dig over the garden, loosening and freeing up the soil for new stuff to grow.

Dance your amazing heart out. With each stamp, clap and wriggle, imagine the yucky stuff being danced away.

Have a good cry. Then wipe your tears away and take your next step.

If writing is your thing, then try a brain drain and dump all that stuff whirring round your head onto the page. Grab a pen, something to write on (remembering to ask politely if the closest thing to you is an animate object) and write it all out.

Start with the first thing that comes to you and don't stop until it's over. It might not make sense, but that just means you're doing it right. This isn't the grammatically perfect and finely-crafted piece you're accustomed to handing in to your English teacher every week after all…nope, and if it does make sense, then that's okay too. There's no need to read it over, so you may never know if it does or not. The point is that you're creating a funnel for all that chatter to wheeeeeeeee! down like screaming kiddies down a helter-skelter, one after another...Then leave them there, in a heap, and walk away!

> Know that there's an art form that speaks to you and that's the one to choose when you want to express yourself and your emotions. Sculpt, paint, sing, dance...compose yourself!

Become aware of the things that can drain your energy and lower your vibration, and avoid them. These things include...

- Too much TV, video gaming or computer time
- Gossip
- Thinking mean thoughts, about yourself or others
- Staying indoors too long
- Too much sugar, caffeine or other stimulants
- Alcohol is a depressant
- Too many late nights

On the other hand, certain things can boost your energy and raise your vibration. These include...

- Laughing
- Fresh air
- Doing something nice for someone else
- Doing something nice for yourself
- Drinking pure water
- Saying thank you
- Meditation
- Getting enough sleep

Add your own ideas to the list and explore what does it for you!

The poet Byron wrote, 'If I don't write to empty my mind, I go mad!' and being a creative and supposedly generous sort of chap, I'm sure he wouldn't mind us playing about with this a bit. Consider the creative activities you like and fill in the gap with whatever works for you!

'If I don't ....to empty my mind, I go mad!'

Chapter 18

Wishing On A Star (and that's You, by the way...)

'Go confidently in the direction of your dreams! Live the life you've imagined.'
Thoreau

Snigger. Delicious. Thump.

Say these words out loud and let the sounds show you what they mean. Some words are delicate or gentle, tickling your ears; others are harsher and can rip through things. Some are heavy; some are light enough to float away.

Mother Theresa, a woman known for her strength, compassion and good sense once said, 'kind words can be short and easy to speak, but their echoes are truly endless'; so a word can make you smile, or just as easily, a word can wound you so deeply that it hurts just remembering and hearing its echo.

Try some out for yourselves. We realise that words don't just affect those who hear them, but the speaker too, as all sounds have an effect on our energy by boosting it, draining it or muddying it up, so choose wisely!

By becoming aware of the energy, or the feeling that words and sounds carry with them we are able to be more choosy, more careful with the words we bandy about. (Some words I have personally longed to use for some time, and lo! here's the perfect chance..!)

Words are incredibly powerful; they're thoughts made into

sound, something more permanent, and written down, they become even stronger. Years ago, only select people were allowed to read or own books because of this power.

So, with that in mind, we recognise that making a list of our dreams, wishes and aspirations is to draw our focus and energy to these thoughts, making them more powerful in the process and more likely to make an appearance in the physical world.

What do you wish for?
It might be anything – a fantastic new outfit for that party; a friend you can really be yourself with; a cool idea for the end of term show; someone to practise guitar with and maybe, yeah, why not! start a band with...

If your wish was to come true, how might your world be different? Are you ready for that kind of change? Spend some time considering this – it'll help you sort out the true heart's desire from the 'I need...!' insatiable desire that is born from unhealthy feelings of lack and is the kind of 'need' that advertisers and those who prey on our insecurities love to focus on.

If you feel you don't have enough, and focus on your 'I need...' place, all your creative energy and desire is going to create more of that for you! More needs and emptinesses that can never be filled.

Change your focus by concentrating your creative powers on more positive outcomes. If you see yourself with whatever it is you want in your life now and if you feel fulfilled and happy as you do this, then go for it!

> Make your wish clear, using as few words as possible and write as if your dream is already a reality, in the present tense...
>
> *I work with a supportive singing teacher... I have an excellent idea for my art project... It is my heart's desire to travel to Brazil... I feel confident enough to really enjoy a drama class before I leave school...*
>
> Write/sing/sew it out, adding *'I dedicate this wish to the highest good of all things'.*
>
> Remember that these wishes should concern you alone. It's never wise to wish change on others as they have their own games to play and tampering with them is not a good idea.

Be aware that anything we focus on really does have a habit of coming to us, and that what you desire may come into being, so be prepared, and as they say, be careful what you wish for.

Writing your wish out into a diary or journal is fine, but here are some other ideas, and of course, being the creative and wonderful being that you totally are, you will come up with your own too!

- Make a wishing line. String a line from one side of your room to the other and peg on your wishes, each on their own piece of paper to flutter in the breeze from a window. Let the air carry your dreams far and wide!

- Create an Aspirafile on your computer, a secret file that contains your deepest desires.

- Hold a seed in your hand, and with your eyes closed, imagine your secret wish becoming part of it. Plant the seed, water and nurture it until your dream blossoms.

• Embroider your dreams onto special cloth. The time and effort you focus on this, you are putting directly into bringing your dream into reality.

• Create a magical box from any material you like. Place your hopes and wishes inside.

• Compose a simple song that contains your wish. Sing it often, or record it!

As a human being, you are an absolutely amazing and magical being, more than capable of bringing more magic into your life. It's true, and we have all been given the essential components to create the very game that we came here to play, and to really enjoy playing it.

Our minds, once they are working for us, are incredible laser-sharp precision machines, able to point our intentions exactly where we want them to go. Our emotions and feelings are perfect indicators of whether something is good for us or not, and they too can work with us as we play to create the game we want.

You know that feeling you get when you're five years old and you see the stocking full of pressies at the bottom of your bed? That rush of Wheeeeeeeeee! Santa's been! See if you can recreate that fizz and buzz of excitement now. Go!

That's right, smell those tangerines, hear the rustle and rip of the wrapping and the whoops of joy as you discover the gold coins, tear the bag and shower them all over the room...

If Christmas doesn't do it for you, chose another special occasion or memory to go to. Really feel it with all of your senses as if it were happening right now!

The more you focus on a desire, the more energy you give it in the form of thoughts and feelings, the more likely it is to become reality.

So now, shut your eyes and with the same vibrancy that you tapped into when you remembered your special day, imagine that your wish has come true – you're holding the acceptance letter in your hands; you've just scored the most fantastic goal; you're leaving the room having just given a fantastic presentation and all your friends are coming up to congratulate you.

See and feel your life as if your wish is reality.

Allow yourself to daydream about how it is and absolutely feel the sensation of joy/excitement/pride in your body.

When you're done, take some of those deep breaths into your belly to ground yourself again in this time and place, knowing – really believing – that your dream is out there, getting closer!

Ensuring that you are well grounded and centred in your body as much of the time as possible will mean that you are more likely to be in tune with what would be the right wish for you. The Universe likes harmony, and wants you to be as much You as you were always intended to be, so if you have a desire that goes along with that, a true heart's desire, you'd better believe that the Universe will support you – all sorts of magic may start to happen at this point!

Flyers start arriving through the post on the subject of your dreams, people suggest ideas to you without you having told them anything about your plans, books in the library on related subjects draw you to them by suddenly appearing irresistible and shiny, and if you take no notice, will throw themselves off shelves into your arms! It's then up to you to take the practical steps and put things into action.

Try it and see what happens for you. Absolutely expect things to go your way and remind yourself often that your dream, or something even better, is coming into being, manifesting right now!

A good time to focus on your heart's desire is before you go to sleep at night. Allow yourself to relax and let go of the day with some big out breaths and bring your plan gently to mind.

Sweet dreams!

Chapter 19

The Fun Starts Here

'To live is just so startling that it leaves little time for anything else.'
Emily Dickinson

So, how does it feel to be playing your game now?

If you've been practising and doing the short exercises, take a moment to consider the effect your doing them has had on your life. We know when something is having a positive effect because we feel better, things seem easier, and life feels, well, just more fun.

Which exercises work for you?

What do you find really useful?

Is there an exercise you want to practise more?

Life really is a game – a gorgeous, challenging, hilarious game that teaches us how to enjoy being ourselves, here on this beautiful Earth if we let it. Once we realise that it's all a game, and then we learn a few basic, simple exercises that can help us to remember this, we become a conscious player, rather than one who is out there on the pitch, not knowing why they're there and becoming more and more confused by everyone shouting and waving their arms about, telling them to run here, keep still, catch this, tackle that...

You are exactly as you were always meant to be.

How does it feel to hear that? Better still, look at yourself in the mirror and say out loud, 'I am exactly right as I am.'

And this isn't about suddenly becoming 'perfect' and never needing to grow or develop or learn anything new; it's about accepting – no, let's go for it, *celebrating* who you are, you gorgeous, beautiful, creative, amazing individual!

Remember to say these positive things to yourself as often as possible, and if ever you start putting yourself down, stop, and gently remind yourself, 'I am doing my best!' and take it from there.

We all play better with a bit of practice, so remember some of the exercises we've tried along the way...

- Breathe *(chapter 4)*
- Keep it simple – clear the clutter *(chapter 3)*
- Meditate and spend some time in stillness *(chapters 4 & 5)*
- Clear your energy body and create a shield *(chapter 8)*
- Relax before sleep *(chapter 5)*
- Listen to your true voice *(chapter 6)*
- Transform your fears *(chapter 12)*
- Set your intentions *(chapter 15)*
- Release stuck energy *(chapters 16 & 17)*
- Bring your dreams to life *(chapter 18)*

And remember to...

- Dig deep and look beneath the surface
- Ask 'Why am I doing this?' from time to time
- Choose for yourself
- Say 'Thank You!' for the good stuff
- Enjoy!

You are exactly as you were always meant to be in this moment, and you now have a few tricks up your sleeve to help you play your amazing game to its fullest.

As we've seen, we create the game we play from moment to moment, so why not play a game where the world and the universe, as you experience it, is a friendly, creative, fun place for you to be?

Just imagine.

Introducing the Greatest Show on Earth...

Hello there, and welcome to **Play The Game**! The show that invites you to Take Your Turn and, come on, audience, yes, that's right! *(Audience shouts, as one)* 'Have A Go!!!'

Yes! It's time to make some choices here, folks! *(Dramatic music as host raises one cheeky eyebrow at audience)*

Just what is it that you want to do? You've come this far, and believe me, ladies and gentlemen, just getting this far through this show takes some guts!

(Pause for chuckles all round)

But seriously now, *(host assumes grave expression)* putting yourself in the spotlight is really something, and only *you* can decide to do it. You have to make this choice on your own.

No looking at anyone else for help on this one.

You can stop here, leave exactly as you are – you've had a fair old time, and I'll even throw in a signed photo or two of yours truly. *(Teeth flashing, host winks hugely at camera).* Not a bad choice, I'm sure you'll agree, though it wouldn't really make much of a show! Ha!

Or, and this is the Big One, ladies and gentlemen, one of you can take the chance to Really Be Yourself!!!! *(Excited murmurs from audience)*

It's scary, I know. Heaven knows who I really am! But this isn't about me. No sireee. This is about someone out there who has a golden opportunity to really **Play The Game**!!!

Who will it be this time? Where will the spotlight land today? *(Lights dim and spotlight begins to scan audience)* Here we go!

Will it be you, madam? And may I congratulate you on your bold choice of headscarf – the ostrich feather detail, on some other lady, might have been a step too far, but on you, cherie, pure perfection! Or you, sir, in the rather fetching orange tie and those broad lapels?

Aha!! Ladies and gentlemen, pray hush, for it seems the light has fallen on...

YOU.

Acknowledgements

I have absolutely loved writing this book and my heart is full of Thank Yous as I sit here now, writing these last sentences before sending this book on its way and out into the world.

Thank You, my family and friends, my teachers, companions and guides.

In your different ways, you have nourished and encouraged me with humour, patience, wisdom and love.

And Thank You to all the amazing young people I have ever had the pleasure to work with. It has been an honour to share such creative and inspiring times with you and this book has grown from those times.

B O O K S

O is a symbol of the world, of oneness and unity. In different cultures it also means the "eye," symbolizing knowledge and insight. We aim to publish books that are accessible, constructive and that challenge accepted opinion, both that of academia and the "moral majority."

Our books are available in all good English language bookstores worldwide. If you don't see the book on the shelves ask the bookstore to order it for you, quoting the ISBN number and title. Alternatively you can order online (all major online retail sites carry our titles) or contact the distributor in the relevant country, listed on the copyright page.

See our website www.o-books.net for a full list of over 500 titles, growing by 100 a year.

And tune in to myspiritradio.com for our book review radio show, hosted by June-Elleni Laine, where you can listen to the authors discussing their books.

mySpiritRadio